Disability and the Media

Key Concerns in Media Studies

Series Editor: **Andrew Crisell**

Within the context of today's global, digital environment, *Key Concerns in Media Studies* addresses themes and concepts that are integral to the study of media. Concisely written by leading academics, the books consider the historical development of these themes and the theories that underpin them and assess their overall significance, using up-to-date examples and case studies throughout. By giving a clear overview of each topic, the series provides an ideal starting point for all students of modern media.

Published

Paul Bowman *Culture and the Media*

Andrew Crisell *Liveness and Recording in the Media*

Stuart Cunningham, Terry Flew and Adam Swift *Media Economics*

Tim Dwyer *Legal and Ethical Issues in the Media*

Katie Ellis and Gerard Goggin *Disability and the Media*

Gerard Goggin *New Technologies and the Media*

David Hendy *Public Service Broadcasting*

Shaun Moores *Media, Place and Mobility*

Sarah Niblock *Media Professionalism and Training*

Sean Redmond *Celebrity and the Media*

Niall Richardson and Sadie Wearing *Gender and the Media*

Forthcoming

Steve Cross *Religion and the Media*

Brian McNair *News Media*

Monika Metykova *Ethnicity and the Media*

Kate O'Riordan *Science and the Media*

Sue Turnbull *Media Audiences*

Disability and the Media

Katie Ellis
Department of Internet Studies, Curtin University of Technology, Australia

Gerard Goggin
Department of Media and Communications, University of Sydney, Australia

First published 2015 by
PALGRAVE

Palgrave in the UK is an imprint of Macmillan Publishers Limited, registered in England, company number 785998, of 4 Crinan Street, London N1 9XW.

Palgrave Macmillan in the US is a division of St Martin's Press LLC, 175 Fifth Avenue, New York, NY 10010.

Palgrave is a global imprint of the above companies and is represented throughout the world.

Palgrave® and Macmillan® are registered trademarks in the United States, the United Kingdom, Europe and other countries.

ISBN 978-0-230-29320-5   ISBN 978-1-137-50171-4 (eBook)

DOI 10.1007/978-1-137-50171-4

This book is printed on paper suitable for recycling and made from fully managed and sustained forest sources. Logging, pulping and manufacturing processes are expected to conform to the environmental regulations of the country of origin.

A catalogue record for this book is available from the British Library.

Library of Congress Cataloging-in-Publication Data
Ellis, Katie, 1978–
  Disability and the media / Katie Ellis, Gerard Goggin.
    pages   cm. — (Key concerns in media studies)

  1. People with disabilities in mass media.   2. Sociology of disability.
  I. Goggin, Gerard, 1964–   II. Title.
  HV1568.E4453 2015
  305.9′08—dc23   2015013156

For Christopher Newell

Contents

Acknowledgements

We have incurred many debts in the researching and writing of this book, especially to our creative and generous colleagues in the vibrant field of disability studies.

In particular, we dedicate this book to a unique, brilliant, compassionate, and impassioned scholar, ethicist, and activist in the field of disability and media, our dearly beloved, late friend Professor Christopher Newell. A fighter for justice and the good life, his words and example live on, bearing their impress in many lines of this book.

The second great influence on this book is Professor Beth Haller, a pioneering and distinguished figure in media and disability research. Beth was kind enough to read a number of chapters and offer indispensable feedback.

We thank the series editor, Andrew Crisell, for his immediate support for the conception of this book and his incisive comments. We greatly appreciate his unstinting patience, wit, and kindness, as he awaited the eventual advent of the manuscript. At Palgrave, we are grateful to Rebecca Barden for commissioning the title and her colleagues for their forbearance and taking the book to press – especially Nicola Cattini and Lloyd Langman. We also wish to thank three anonymous reviewers of the manuscript for their thoughtful comments, to which we hope we have done justice.

Katie would like to thank colleagues at Murdoch University School of Arts where this project was commenced and colleagues in the Department of Internet Studies at Curtin University where the book was finished, and Mike Kent and Scott Hollier who read chapters, discussed ideas, and offered valuable feedback. She would also like to thank Gerard for the invitation to be part of this project in the first place and the Australia Research Council for awarding her a Discovery Early Career Researcher Award to research, think, and write about disability and the media. Finally, Katie would like to thank her entire family, but Chris and Stella in particular, for their support across the duration of the project.

Gerard would like to thank the University of Sydney, and especially his colleagues in the Department of Media and Communications, for their support. He is also grateful to the Australian Research Council for the privilege of his Future Fellowship (FT130100097) on Disability and Digital Technology, of which this book is an output. Gerard is very grateful to Katie for a great partnership in collaborating on this book and for her great reserves of patience and encouragement in the face of his glacial progress in holding up his end of the bargain. Finally, Gerard thanks Jacqui, Liam, and Bianca for their love and support, and especially their patience and encouragement in the finish.

The authors and publisher thank the copyright holders for permission to reproduce the following:

Articles 1 and 21 from the Convention on the Rights of Persons with Disabilities. Reproduced with the permission of the United Nations. Articles 19, 22, and 27 from the 1948 Declaration of Human Rights. Reproduced with the permission of the United Nations.

1 Introduction: Why Does Disability Matter for Media?

Every day we encounter disability in our lives in some form or other. Many of us live with disability and impairment. Many more have friends, lovers, family, work mates, and acquaintances who experience disability, often without our realizing. Disability is just part of ordinary life. Often it fades into the background. Other times disability emerges as a difference worth discussing or becomes a problem for ourselves, others, and social institutions. In many of the societies, cultures, and groups to which we belong, disability is increasingly 'normal'. It's just part of living in 'super'-diverse – or even pretty homogenous – societies. It has taken a long while for disability to gain the acknowledgement it deserves, and there's a lot to be tackled in terms of equality, social participation, and full cultural citizenship. But what does disability have to do with media? Well, it turns out, as we outline in this book, quite a bit.

Consider a day in the life of many of us. When we walk across the street, whether strolling, pushing a pram or wheelchair, or riding a bike or scooter, we might whiz down a 'curb cut' – the smoothed down bit of the pavement or sidewalk that allows us easy access to the road. Or we might navigate a shopping centre, park, or airport trying to find accessible toilets. In our university or school, we might look out for a hearing loop in the lecture theatre, use a sign language interpreter or person to transcribe lectures or take notes, or use accessible technology to use the Internet.

In various contexts, we are all familiar with the iconic signs that represent 'disabled'. Take, for instance, the classic image of the wheelchair user familiar to people all around the world. This is a white stylized image of a person in a wheelchair, on a blue background. The colours are so widely known that the blue is often referred to as 'handicapped blue'. First devised in 1968 by Danish design student Susanne Koefed, then modified by Karl Montan (who added the circle representing the head of the seated figure) (Ben-Moshea and Powell, 2007), the icon is part of an international standard defining a set of graphic symbols that provide public information in all locations and sectors where the public has access (International Organization for Standardization, 2007, 2013). The International Symbol of Access is used in a wide range of situations where the access is not just about physical access for wheelchair users. Not surprisingly, it has been critiqued by those who argue it excludes as well as enables or includes. A group of US-based designers associated with the Accessible Icon Project have produced an alternative Symbol of Access which aims to signify a more active – rather than passive – image of disability. Such efforts have built on the work of artists such as British-based Caroline Cardus. In partnership with community and disability arts charity Inter-Action MK, Cardus created a 2004 travelling exhibition of alternative disability signs entitled *The Way Ahead* (Disability Arts Online, 2004). These three signs offer alternative ways to understand and communicate about disability than those we customarily encounter.

As this brief discussion indicates, when we examine the taken-for-granted ideas and assumptions about the International Symbol of Access – the most common of all signs of disability – it turns out that disability is much richer, more complex, and more present in everyday life than is generally realized. These symbols of disability are a concrete example of how we communicate about disability. In the kinds of societies across the world today, much communication takes place via media of one sort or another. So it is a very short road from communication to media, when it comes to disability now and into the future.

Even in the poorest countries and societies, media such as radio, television, cinema, music, advertising, and the increasing use of mobile phones form the ways in which billions of the world's people communicate, participate in society, exercise their political rights, make meaning, and create culture. Media has great importance in the contemporary world because it provides the channels, networks, formats, and languages through which much of life takes place and finds meaning. When we inspect the wide diversity of contemporary media, in our particular media worlds, it is surprising how often disability makes an appearance and then, if we care to – and know how to – look more deeply, how foundational disability is to the structuring of media. And, vice versa, how much media is implicated in the shaping of disability. Before we get underway, let's talk first about what we mean by disability and how to define it.

Disability – What Does It Mean?

Disability is often associated with physical impairment – for instance, something that a person is born with or acquires (through a car or work accident, for instance) that makes them permanently disabled. One of the most common images that comes to mind of disability is a person in a wheelchair – so it is no surprise that the International Symbol of Access is exactly this. Such a person, in the past at least, was often described as 'wheelchair-bound'. They may have a condition such as paraplegia or quadriplegia, with loss of bodily functioning due to spinal cord injury. Another common image of disability is a person who has a sensory disability – for instance, someone who is Blind, Deaf, or has a communication disability (for instance, who cannot speak and was formerly described as 'mute'). There are a number of other kinds of disability also widely recognized, such as intellectual disability (formerly associated with 'Down's syndrome'), or autism.

We mention these images because often when disability is encountered these are the ways it is imagined. For us, and many other people now, disability means something quite different. While there is a kernel of truth to these images of disability, not least because they speak to the experience and lives of actual people with disability, they also constitute a major barrier. Such images are, in effect, unhelpful, 'disabling' stereotypes. Such stereotypes of disability are really out of date and inaccurate. And, rather like racist, sexist, national, class, or homophobic stereotypes, they distort social reality – constituting a real barrier not only to understanding but also to the transformation of society that is really needed to embrace disability, not reject it out of fear and loathing.

Fortunately, we now have better, more accurate, and fairer ways to define and understand disability. Let's start with the widely accepted international definition called the International Classification of Functioning, Disability and Health (ICF). In 2001, this definition was adopted by all 191 countries who are 'member states' of the World Health Organization (WHO). While still problematic, the definition is a step forward in how disability is understood. Firstly, it is an interactive, dynamic definition of disability: 'A person's functioning or disability is conceived as a dynamic interaction between health conditions and environmental and personal factors' (WHO, 2001: 8). Both functioning and disability are 'multidimensional' (WHO, 2001: 8). Secondly, disability is the 'umbrella term for any or all of: an impairment of body structure or function, a limitation in activities, or a restriction in participation'

(WHO, 2001: 8). So when the classification is broken down further, it is under the following headings:

- body functions and body structures;
- activities and participation; and
- environmental factors.

The first two of these, body functions and structures, most resemble the way that disability has been understood in recent time – as something to do with impairments, defects, or health issues that affect the body.

So this first element of the classification includes eight different kinds of body functions: mental functions; sensory functions; pain; voice and speech functions; functions of cardiovascular and other systems; functions of digestive, metabolic, and endocrine systems; genitourinary and reproductive systems; and neuromusculoskeletal and movement-related functions. The second element lists eight matching body structures, starting with structures of the nervous system; eye, ear, and related structures; structures involved in voice and speech; and so on.

At this point, you are probably thinking that you have wandered into a medical or health sciences lecture, perhaps no problem for a student studying to be a doctor or disability professional, but what does it have to do with media?

This is where the third and fourth elements of the classification give us a clue. Here activities are brought into the picture: learning and applying knowledge; tasks; communication; mobility; self-care; interpersonal interactions and relationships; and community, social, and civic life. And then are the environmental factors that affect disability, such as products and technology; natural and human-made environments; support and relationships; attitudes; services, systems and policies.

So what emerges from this ICF definition is that disability is not just a medical or health condition. Disability involves the interaction among our bodies, activities, societies, and environments. This ICF definition has been adopted by many governments (not all) and is often used in the gathering of official statistics on disability. This definition provided the conceptual framework for the most authoritative international report on disability, the first *World Report on Disability*, undertaken by WHO with the World Bank and released in 2011.

The *World Report on Disability* gave the following global estimates of prevalence of disability (based on two WHO surveys from 2002 to 2004). It estimated that 2.9% of the world's population could be regarded as having severe disability. Further, that 15.3% of the world's population could be seen as having moderate and severe disability. The figures vary by region and country and also by gender. Women overall were estimated to have a higher prevalence of disability – 11%, not least because of the higher number of older women in the population than older men (World Health Organization, 2011: 7). Measuring disability is a very complex, problematic, and hotly debated area, so for brevity we will leave the figures and disputes here and instead return to the discussion of how disability is defined, and why this is highly relevant for the understanding of media.

As the *World Report on Disability* outlines:

> Disability is the umbrella term for impairments, activity limitations and participation restrictions, referring to the negative aspects of the interaction between an individual (with a health condition) and that individual's contextual factors (environmental and personal factors). (World Health Organization, 2011: 4)

At the outset, the report notes the importance of improving social participation by 'addressing the barriers which hinder persons with disabilities in their day to day lives' (World Health Organization, 2011: 4). The report points out that a 'person's environment has a huge impact on the experience and extent of disability' (World Health Organization, 2011). In particular, it reports that 'inaccessible environments create disability by creating barriers to participation and inclusion' (World Health Organization, 2011). The report illustrates environment barriers with three examples:

- a Deaf individual without a sign language interpreter
- a wheelchair user in a building without an accessible bathroom or elevator
- a blind person using a computer without screen-reading software. (World Health Organization, 2011: 7)

Interestingly, the first example has to do with language, and the third example has to do with the defining media of our time – computers and software. The report also goes on to note that 'knowledge and attitudes are important environmental factors':

> Raising awareness and challenging negative attitudes are often first steps towards creating more accessible environments for persons with disabilities. Negative imagery and language, stereotypes, and

stigma – with deep historic roots – persist for people with disabilities around the world. (World Health Organization, 2011: 7)

Here we arrive at the heartland territory for media students, teachers, workers, and researchers. The media is paramount for awareness-raising, attitude formation, circulation of ideas, personal expression, social identity, and cultural currency. If disability is not just medical, or psychological, but also a mix of these with the social, then at a deep level it involves that great organ of the social – the media.

Social (Disability) Media

So let us pause at this point, in order to summarize, draw out, and discuss some of the implications of the definition of disability.

To start with, it is clear from the WHO report, as well as from nationally available statistics and research, that depending on the definition adopted people with disabilities number a surprisingly large portion of populations (often estimated at 20% in some Western countries). Disability is also highly heterogeneous and diverse: people can have intellectual impairment, mental health problems, physical or sensory impairments, degenerative illnesses, and so on. Disability is not just one thing. And disabilities often interact with each other to produce complex, unstable, changing conditions. So there are lots of big and little differences in disability, which means that people with disabilities cannot all be approached in the same way. Disability is dynamic: people can be born with impairments, acquire them, have them from time to time, and, if we live long enough, we will all surely count as disabled. So disability changes over the course of each person's life. The nature of disability is often shape-shifting and hard to pin down.

For all these reasons, and a few more, polarizing people into 'us' (people with disabilities) or 'them' (those without disabilities) is surprisingly hard to do. Actually, so too is declaring that there are those of us who are truly disabled (and deserving), and those who are able-bodied.

Most people, after all, have some sort of crutch, support, helping technology, bodily variation, impairment, infirmity, or weakness. The most common technology of disability, it is often said, is a pair of glasses (not the wheelchair).

Add to which, disability also takes on different meanings and implications across different social, cultural, and linguistic communities. In Britain, for instance, 'disabled' people is the preferred term, whereas in the United States and elsewhere, it is more widely accepted usage to speak of 'people with disabilities'. 'Crip' is a time-honoured term of abuse, but it's also now been reclaimed by people with disabilities – not least in terms like 'crip theory', the title of one of the most famous recent US academic books on disability (McRuer, 2006).

Yet while disability takes very different forms, there are also many aspects common to the experience of the different groups and individuals with disabilities. To hazard a generalization, common experiences often revolve around exclusion, discrimination, oppression, and inequality in work and income. People with disabilities tend to have a lower income, poor access to education, lower levels of participation in society, and are often still segregated from mainstream society via specialized institutions.

To grasp this complex yet common phenomenon, we need to go further in thinking about disability and understanding its social, political, and cultural dimensions. In unpacking the ICF definition, we have noted the emerging consensus that disability is not just a medical or health problem that deserves 'special' attention. As we will discuss later, this is a view summed up as the 'medical model' of disability. Instead, it is crucial to understand that disability is formed through social, cultural, political, and other dimensions of life. This view of disability, as we will discover, is often referred to as the 'social model' (although it involves a wide range of other philosophies of disability too). Part of the point of the 2001 ICF definition is trying to strike a balance between the 'medical' and 'social' models of disability. The *World Report on Disability* takes this international understanding and definition of disability into a much deeper exploration of its social, cultural, and political conditions.

Central to this process is the role played in defining disability by people with disabilities themselves. As WHO itself emphasizes, the contemporary definition of disability is not settled – it is evolving. The other key international frame of reference that puts people with disabilities and the achievement of justice and freedom for all of us when it comes to disability is the 2006 United Nations *Convention on the Rights of Persons with Disabilities* (CRPD). The CRPD provides the first unequivocal international recognition of the oppressive situation of people with disabilities, specifically that basic human rights are routinely denied to the world's disabled. This Convention enjoins, and indeed requires, the governments of the world that are signatories to take action to safeguard the human rights of persons with disabilities. The provisions of the Convention should be henceforth distributed to all schoolchildren and committed to our memories, but, for the present, let us recite only Article 1:

The purpose of the present Convention is to promote, protect and ensure the full and equal enjoyment of all human rights and fundamental freedoms by all persons with disabilities, and to promote respect for their inherent dignity.

Persons with disabilities include those who have long-term physical, mental, intellectual or sensory impairments which in interaction with various barriers may hinder their full and effective participation in society on an equal basis with others.

As this book unfolds, we will further explore the deceptively simple yet richly complicated concept of disability now put firmly on the international and national agenda by the CRPD and the other documents we have discussed. However, before we head to this terrain, let us consider the various objections disability often raises – and that you, the reader, might share at this point.

It is certainly the case that there are many people who would wish to call the whole concept of disability into question. Many feel that to describe someone as 'disabled' is not only to put that person in a kind of ghetto but also to treat as categorical what is only relative. Aren't we all disabled, in the sense that some of us, though pretty smart in some areas, are physically gauche, or hopeless at ball games, or poor at maths? And so isn't it better to talk, as some do, about being 'differently abled'. If so, where would this leave our idea of disability? Indeed, what kind of disability are we discussing here?

In response to objections such as these, it is important to develop a more nuanced argument about why disability is still the central concept to grasp this phenomenon (though it is a notion that comes replete with its problems and limitations). After all, disability does indeed touch all, or at least most, of our lives – though, as we've been suggesting, not as typically still understood.

We can start with the idea that disability is what society makes of it in response to the experience and fears of impairments in human bodies and minds. These are the frameworks, myths, and power relations that form our social perceptions. Such an idea is embodied in the influential 'social model' of disability advanced by British activists and theorists such as Mike Oliver. Briefly put, the social model holds that there is a binary between 'impairment' (for instance, the material, bodily experience of being blind or deaf) and 'disability' (the barriers that society creates around certain impairments). Having an impairment does not in itself mean that someone is incapable of functioning, living, or participating in society – it is more the case that society, routinely, as a reflex, 'disables' people.

In society today, disability's cultural work of negotiating difference and 'enforcing normalcy' (Davis, 1995) involves the media as a vitally important arena. Powerful ideas about disability are circulated via the media. Key ideas and beliefs about normalcy, health, our bodies and identities – and indeed the nature of life itself (and when it should be commenced or ended) – pervade and structure media, and through this are deeply embedded governing assumptions in culture itself. Disability, then, is a key concern in media – so what are some concrete ways in which this plays out?

A Day of Media with Disability

To briefly evoke some sense of the vast landscape of disability and media, try this exercise. Keep a diary of your media consumption for a day (or better still, a week) and make of a note of each occurrence of disability-related material.

Everyone's media diary will be different, but here's one possible (if not typical) journal. The first things people often notice are news and current affairs items about people with disabilities. As we wrote this introductory chapter, our attention was captured by a new item reporting that one of our music heroes, the folk-rock blues-harp player Jim Conway, boarded his plane – but the airline refused to assist him to transfer from his wheelchair to his seat (Visentin, 2014). Another item included a nightly news bulletin covering an item on a new Medical Research Future Fund with exciting possibilities for curing disability and disease (Law, 2014). In the UK press, we heard more about the cuts to welfare entitlements for unemployed people with disabilities (Butler, Taylor, and Bell, 2013) – something which echoes around the world, where eligibility tests for benefits are often being 'tightened' to encourage the disabled and other unemployed to seek and find work (Ireland, 2014). On a seemingly positive note, there are many 'inspirational', 'uplifting' stories about 'overcoming' disability on websites, complete with videos, such as that of young Mexican lawyer Adriana Macias, born without arms, whose credo is that there is 'no obstacle to success in life – positive attitude is the essential tool to achieve individual and collective projects' (Disability in Action, 2014). So far, so good. There is plenty of media material on people with disabilities, just in the daily news. But what if we dig deeper, and look a little farther afield.

When we turn on the television, download television programmes, or watch TV or video on our Internet or mobile devices, for entertainment, there's a wealth of media we could tag as disability-related. It is not just television shows about people with disabilities. There is some of that, but not a lot. Although, many series do have one or two characters, and there are increasing numbers of programmes that focus on disability (Rodan, Ellis, and Lebeck, 2014; Ellis, 2015). In crime dramas, the appeal often comes from eccentric, quirky, 'defective detectives' – crime-solving characters, whose disability (from physical impairments and blindness, through autism, to psychological, mental health, or episodic conditions) is part of how their creators present them as different and interesting. In new 'cult TV' series like *Orange Is the New Black* or *Breaking Bad*, we find that the most interesting portrayals of disability are not the most obvious ones – but that they are central to the plot and conception of the show. A narrative kicks into action, for instance, because of a character's invisible or barely visible, as well as very obvious, disability. Much the same applies to cinema. In the movies, with their relatively long duration, disability is often the key subject for exploration.

By now, our media diaries should be bulging with disability-inflected examples. If we turn to the dynamic, fast-moving environment of digital media, there are even more significant examples of disability to be encountered. And many of these instances of disability in digital media require us, even more so, to set aside and rethink our preconceptions. Consider, for instance, that for many people with disability digital media provides – sometimes for the first time – opportunities to access, consume, and make media. Smartphones and tablets are often discussed – not unproblematically, we hasten to add – as a 'revolution' in media for many groups of people with disabilities, whether people with intellectual disabilities, or Deaf–Blind people. By the courtesy of the Internet, social and mobile media technologies, including blogs, YouTube, Facebook, Twitter, and a wide range of other platforms around the world (less familiar to English-speaking audiences), all of us can easily encounter material produced by 'produsers' with disability (amateur users who produce content). Some of this material is not so obviously about disability, but rather is produced through communication by people with disabilities – sometimes with other people with disabilities, sometimes with people who might or not identify as disabled.

A fair portion of disability-related material in digital media is very offensive. It's insulting, rude, bigoted, threatening, and hateful. Unfortunately, this really awful – at times shocking – media about disability is not just a social media rant. Discriminatory, offensive, violent attitudes and actions, and social exclusion are the daily experience of many people with disabilities, offline as well as online. Without exaggerating the importance of the media – and falling into the trap of being too 'media-centric' (Morley, 2009; Hepp, 2013) – the appearance of super-offensive material in our disability media diary exercise brings something important out in the open. It reminds us of a central issue in disability, media, and society: while things have transformed significantly, in many ways there is great injustice remaining and much to do. Let us briefly explore this contradiction with a case study of a prominent media celebrity; in the final section of this introductory chapter, we give a brief overview of the book's approach, organization, and topics.

Dwarfing Disability

At the widely watched 2013 MTV Music Video Awards, the thing that went viral was the spectacle of 20-year-old musician, actor, and entertainer Miley Cyrus making 'twerking' a household name. In the wake of her performance, an extraordinary wave of sustained criticism irrupted in the blogosphere and mainstream media. Cyrus was variously accused of racism (Ninjacate, 2013), hyper sexualization of young girls (Briggs, 2013), presented as proof positive that mainstream media was implicated in a discourse of 'slut shaming' (Dries, 2013) – evidence that the music industry had lost its progressive edge (Freeman, 2013). Sexism and racism are two of the most prominent, popular as well as scholarly, topics in discussions of the media. Given the outcry, and microscopic attention subsequently paid to Miley Cyrus' work, it's odd that her follow-up performance on German TV, just a few days later, escaped public attention.

Cyrus appeared on the German television show *Schlag Den Raab*, a live game show (the English version of the format is *Beat the Star*). She was joined by a 'troupe of little people providing backing vocals, playing instruments and dancing to the number' (MTV, 2013; News.Com.Au, 2013). Cyrus spanked a dwarf backup dancer, 'who was clad in a pair of holographic silver leggings' (MTV, 2013) as she twerked to *We Can't Stop* (2013). It could be argued that this incident took Cyrus unawares, except she did tweet a picture of herself with the troupe immediately after the show (Cyrus, 2013). Add to which, a few days later Cyrus performed with the same dancer at the Sony Music Awards in London (Smart, 2013). The British *Sun* saw the incident as Cyrus being a try hard: 'Miley Cyrus is running out of maximum publicity boxes to tick. She's managed nudity, on-stage sex simulation – and now dwarf antics' (Smart, 2013).

In late November 2013, some two weeks later, Cyrus was the head-line at the after-party of the American Music Awards, where two dwarves were also hired to 'recreate her ironic twerking performance from the MTV video awards'. Captured in an Instagram video, one dancer was dressed in Miley's signature rabbit costume while the other wore a 'Robin Thicke-inspired striped suit' (Robertson, 2013). Entertainment media hosts raised the question whether this latest twerking turn was 'too much' (Hollywood Life, 2013), but some online commenters took a different view. Take, for instance, Ty33Budd, who contended:

> People are offended by the interaction of the little people because they for some reason feel 'sorry' for little people, but I'm sure if you ask a little person, they wouldn't mind at all, because its publicity to show that they can do everything that we can do, they are crippled or disadvantaged humans, they are just smaller. (https://www.youtube.com/watch?v=wjWmShKSh6M)

Another online commentator, Mattspinaze, quipped 'Hi Ho Hi Ho It's off Twerk we go...', a sentiment echoed in a parody photo on Twitter (@Uncle_A_Trotter, 2013).

In the main, however, most negative comments were not preoccupied with Cyrus' dwarf performances but just criticized her publicity strategies or cut straight to the pervasive online commentary genre of vile sexist abuse: 'she is a whore, slut, and cheap dancer'. Perhaps media and consumers were experiencing fatigue with both Miley and the tired debates on her persona and performance. Or, as we suspect, perhaps the use of dwarfs as backup dancers just did not seem as offensive due to a long, and largely unquestioned, cultural fascination with 'little people'. In any case, the incidents attracted little mainstream discussion about disability issues – until Hollis Jane, one of Cyrus' dancers, spoke out on her blog:

> I was a bear in Miley Cyrus' VMA performance and it was my first time doing anything like that... anything where I was being used because of my height, not because of my talent. And I will be the first one to tell you that standing on that stage, in that costume was one

of the most degrading things I felt like I could ever do. I realize not everyone shares my opinion and I might just be young and naive, but I feel like the acceptance of this kind of treatment has got to stop. (Jane, 2013)

Jane's blog post was covered in *Huffington Post* (Blumberg, 2013) and a range of other media outlets internationally. It drew some vitriolic responses on Jane's own blog:

Ugly little midget. Of course you'd whine and cry AFTER receiving payment. Who would want to see you act in a major film along side a well known actor? Honestly, unless you're cast in a comedy you shouldn't be on the big screen. At least if you're in a comedy I won't feel so bad laughing at a hideous midget aka you! You remind me of a cockroach/owl hybrid.. ugly!...Enjoy your 15 minutes of fame, I guess using the internet for sympathy is the only way you'd get noticed besides people gawking at your midget self. Jude M. (Various, 2013)

Such abuse certainly abounds in contemporary online media, where participatory digital culture has long been acknowledged to have its highly visible dark side. Like much of the abuse that surfaces and structures Internet cultures, there is a deep set of dynamics associated with disability and the media that make Miley's twerking with dwarves the tip of the iceberg. Consider, for instance, the long histories of how people of short stature are regarded and stereotyped as freaks. This involves the contradictory, intertwined emotions of both fascination (Cyrus' dancing with dwarves) and its flipside hatred (abuse of 'midgets').

On 11th February 1863, some 150 years earlier, the *New York Times* devoted one full page of its eight-page publication to the wedding of a famous freak show performer, Charles Sherwood Stratton (a.k.a. General Tom Thumb), and his bride-to-be, Mercy Lavinia Warren Bump (Bogdan, 1990). Titled 'The Loving Lilliputians', the article told of the high society event and Stratton's and Warren's early childhoods, average height parents, and their discovery by Freak Show entrepreneur Mr Bauman (1863). As Bogdan suggests, the couple's wedding festivities were major media events of their time, something that 'distracted' Americans from the Civil War. Tickets were sold to the event (Bogdan, 1990) with as many as 20,000 people missing out (1863). The interest in the wedding drew on a long cultural fascination with dwarves, skilfully stage-managed by Bauman.

During the second half of the twentieth century, the rise of television and movies as dominant sources of entertainment saw the decline of live-entertainment freak shows as a separate genre in their right, as they came to be regarded as vulgar and exploitative (Gerber, 1996). Despite this genteel distaste, dwarfs continue to be exhibited in the newer electronic media – notably, in the popular 1990s movie *Austin Powers* and, more recently, the reality TV show *The Littlest Groom*. Strikingly new kinds of freak shows have emerged in popular culture – for instance, in bars and venues with the rise of event entertainment such as dwarf tossing and dwarf bowling. The involvement of short people in such shows was featured in the 2013 film *The Wolf of Wall Street* where a brokerage film at the height of its speculative excess in the 1980s hires a dwarf entertainer as part of its weekly rewards for sale executives (Scorsese, 2013). Distinguished British disability scholar Tom Shakespeare argues that dwarfs have been subject to a 'comedy model of disability' whereby they have been disparaged and ridiculed — identifying a number of Facebook pages dedicated to the disablement of people with this impairment (Shakespeare, 2009).

So, when we stumble upon the popular depiction and fascination with dwarves in contemporary media, and then analyse it further, we find it raises strikingly uncomfortable questions about the place of disability in the media and indeed wider culture. That such disturbing, cruel, and outdated images of, and attitudes towards, people persist is not just restricted to dwarves. It is a widespread, entrenched way of seeing disability in society. Media not only matter, in their pervasiveness and power; they play an important role in the power relations and shaping of disability.

Disability and the Media – The Current State of Play

We hope that we have given a clear sense by now why we think the concept of disability is needed – and remains a useful, analytically adequate, and highly relevant concept. Without the critical concept of disability – as is also the case with gender, race, or sexuality – we lack a way to understand how society came to be, to what extent it has transformed, and to what extent still, regrettably, disability structures the lives of disabled and (temporarily) non-disabled people. Indeed, we lack fundamental insight into what makes us human (and inhuman).

In making this argument, we are sympathetic to the idea that disability should not be a ghetto and that people's lives don't just revolve around their disability. However, it is true that, for many people, the choice to what extent they focus upon, disregard, celebrate, or feel ashamed about, forget, or are nonchalant about their disability is taken out of their hands, because they are in effect still kept in real or de facto ghettos – be it in the institutions that exist to hold and manage people with disabilities or in the discriminatory practices that many face at the hands of the 'caring' professions – from special education, through to social work, to health and medicine – that control their lives. Thus, we all live with various shortcomings, impairments, things we can or cannot do, or things we could do if we had the right support, resources, genes, life circumstance, or experiences – and disability usefully draws attention to, and broadens our understanding of, these differences. However, the multifaceted yet real phenomenon of disability also has powerful effects on the lives of disabled people, and their friends and families, that are quite distinct and troubling, and pose particular challenges.

It is with this sense of the long road still to be travelled in relation to disability and society – and the central role that media plays in this – that this book has been conceived. In what follows, we aim to critically introduce the complex relationship between disability and the media. We consider key questions such as: How is the social position of people with disability influenced by the media? Does the media adequately reflect the lives of people with disability or perpetuate stigma against them? Or both? What is the relevance of disability guidelines? Are people with disability denied access to the media, both physically and culturally? What are the deep cultural underpinnings of disability in contemporary media? Is a disability culture reflected in the media? What is the potential of new digital technologies and cultures to establishing a more diverse, rich, and just media?

The primary audience for this book is clearly academic, especially students and teachers. We hope that researchers will also be attracted to the book: both researchers from disability studies, where there is a wave of younger and emerging scholars who take media as a natural site for inquiry, as well as media, communication, and cultural studies, where there is great need and potential yet slow development of work on disability.

Besides students, teachers, and researchers, we have also written this book to broadly appeal to readers with specific interests and investments in disability. This includes non-profit disability organizations across health, welfare, education, and rights; policymakers with an interest in disability policy; and disability advocates and activists.

Furthermore, from our own experience, we are keenly attuned to the fact that there is still a need for topical books about disability among lay readers, including people with disabilities themselves and their families and friends. This is evidenced by the vibrant way in which disability is emerging in public culture, yet still there is a lack of good books about some aspects of disability.

Media is a highly significant part of contemporary society and culture, and, as we argue here, it is therefore key to understanding disability. We seek to draw upon the best theoretical work and research on disability internationally, and throughout the book will offer analysis and examples of disability across topical media of news, the press, broadcasting, and new media in particular. This approach is important. Although disability is a burgeoning area of academic publishing, where there is a great appetite for new books and there are a significant number of very good theoretical and research works, there are very few – if any – that consider the media. Of course, our book builds upon an extensive body of work that is important to briefly outline here (not least to provide a handy list for interested readers).

Around the world, disability studies is booming – both as a new discipline in its own right, often referred to as critical disability studies, and as an interdisciplinary field in which a very wide range of scholars participate from diverse disciplines across humanities and social sciences, and indeed all other areas of sciences (Watson, Roulstone and Thomas, 2014). While disability studies is vibrant, urgent, and burgeoning, there has been much less work and action in the area of media and disability – though this is now changing.

There is a steady stream of papers; however, overall there is still a surprisingly small amount of research literature to be found across all journals on disability and media. Stranger still, available papers cluster around particular topics; for instance, analysis of the representation of aspects of disability in print media. The literature thus far leaves much to do with media and disability unscrutinized and is especially lacking when it comes to sustained, longitudinal, comparative, or large-scale studies.

That said, *Disability and the Media* certainly draws upon the papers that form this research literature on disability and media. We are also especially indebted to the few pioneering book-length studies, such as Martin Norden's 1994 classic *Cinema of Isolation* (Norden, 1994); Cumberbatch and Negrine's *Images of Disability on Television* (Cumberbatch and Negrine, 1992); and Pointon and Davies classic *Framed: Interrogating Disability in the Media* (Pointon and Davies, 1997).

Charles A. Riley's *Disability and the Media: Prescriptions for Change* is an obvious predecessor to ours, with a neater fit (Riley, 2005). Riley's book is based on the author's experience as a co-founder of the US disability lifestyle magazine and multimedia group, *We*, and advocates reforms aimed at media practitioners and industry. Riley's treatment is very much rooted in the US context of disability and media, and, in his own words, is often 'relentlessly negative' (p. xviii) and suggests depictions of disability have not really changed since the 1920s. We certainly share Riley's frustration and experience of the glacial change in this area. However, both the present conjuncture and our focus differ markedly, as we seek to acknowledge and analyse the diverse and complex representations of disability as well as the stereotypes.

Long-term US journalism educator and media studies Professor Beth Haller's *Representing Disability in an Ableist World: Essays on Mass Media* (Haller, 2010) is a capstone to her comprehensive, dedicated, and pioneering body of work. Haller's book is an important set of essays that not only recognizes the stigmatizing history the media has with disability but also celebrates the potential of new media forms and disability culture. We draw extensively on Haller's work (including her many papers and vibrant social media presence) as her research provides the best evidence available not only on the limited ways the media depicts disability but also on the potential of the media to offer a diversity of representation.

The two other notable, dedicated books on disability and the media are written by one of us – Katie Ellis's *Disability and Popular Culture* (Ellis, 2015) and her co-authored book *Disability, Obesity and Ageing* (Rodan, Ellis and Lebeck, 2014).

Much energy in research, critique, policy, practice, and design has come from the area of new media and technology. We have each written, with other collaborators, two key books in this area. Katie Ellis and Mike Kent's *Disability and New Media* (Ellis and Kent, 2011) focuses upon new media and questions of accessibility and design, and it is an attempt to build on Gerard Goggin and Christopher Newell's 2003 examination of the ways new media technologies stigmatize rather than liberate people with disability in *Digital Disability: The Social Construction of Disability in New Media* (Goggin and Newell, 2003a). *Disability and the Media* not only takes up these important concerns of our previous work and that of other scholars working on disability and technology but also explores participation and representation to offer a general introduction to media – old and new, commercial, public service, and community, alternative and emergent, formal and informal.

In this book, more than anything, we wish to fill the gap for a general book on disability and media that takes a comprehensive view, albeit in the case of a very short introduction. As we have noted, there are books, research papers, and policy reports on particular aspects of disability and media, yet despite these invaluable available accounts, what is clear is that many important aspects of disability and media are neglected. So in what lies ahead we'll try to introduce and address these concerns in an integrated and accessible way.

Overview of the Book

In this book, then, we aim to provide a concise and integrated account of disability and media that offers a road map to the key areas of participation, access, representation, and the potential for social inclusion and exclusion.

Chapter 2, 'Understanding Disability and Media', explores the significance of culture, disability, and the media, highlighting their interconnections. The chapter lays the foundation for the book by defining the social, medical, and cultural models of disability. Chapter 3, 'Media's Role in Disability', sketches a theory of disability and the media, beginning firstly with the question of access. We consider the importance of different forms of media, such as radio for the Blind, or closed captioning on television enabling access for people who are Deaf. Indeed, the availability of Braille is reframed as a media access issue. Finally, the chapter considers the emergence of newer technologies such as digital television and Internet technologies to explore whether they have followed the disabling trajectory of the introduction of older media.

From the question of access, we move on to the crucial topic of representation in Chapter 4, 'The News on Disability'. While people with disabilities are constituted in particular, often different ways, as media audiences, consumers, and users, how are they imagined by media forms, languages, narratives, conventions, and programmes? The case of the news is an excellent place to discern the representation of disability because it reveals the stereotypes, myths, and images of disability that may be found across a range of media forms. In this chapter, we analyse how disability figures in what is regarded as news, and how reporters and journalists refer to disability and interact with people with disabilities as sources, celebrities, victims. We look at the perceived problems in how disability is reported, the inadequacy of 'guidelines' to deal with the issues raised, and suggest how questions of ethics, responsibility, objectivity, and truth may be reframed. The chapter draws upon case studies of news and disability taken from political reporting, current affairs, health and science news, and sports media.

In Chapter 5, 'Beyond Disabled Broadcasting', we continue the discussion of representation but apply it specifically to popular television media. The chapter examines how disability figures across the various formats and programmes common to broadcast television, with specific case studies derived from a number of television genres. We examine the ways disability is represented in these formats and programmes to shape narrow ideas about normalcy as well as signal towards prospects for change. We also consider the salience of more diverse representations of disability. Finally, we argue that while there is some evidence of incorporation of disabled characters, actors, presenters, themes, and awareness into mainstream television, what is most interesting is the development of innovative programmes that take up and engage with new ideas in disability, and indeed what can be called 'disability culture'. Chapter 6, 'Disability and Media Work', draws on the concept of community media to consider the trends in training and employment of people with disabilities in the media. We note that while change is slow in mainstream media industries, there have been notable exceptions at the community level. The chapter also considers the great prospects and already demonstrated innovation in the ways that individuals and groups with disabilities have taken up opportunities to use new digital, informal media to create new kinds of public spheres.

The conclusion to the book, 'Doing Justice to Disability and Media', argues that long-standing questions of the role and responsibility of the media to provide balance, objectivity, accurate information, adequate narratives, and imagination for democratic societies can be enhanced by considering disability. A critical understanding not only allows us to appreciate how media representations of disability are highly normative and influential for fundamental ideas of ourselves, our relationships with each other, what is normal, and how society is constructed, but it also calls upon us to deepen our ideas of media diversity, and what this might mean.

2 Understanding Disability and Media

Contemporary understandings of disability have significantly altered. As we have outlined in Chapter 1, there are various reasons behind this new dispensation of disability, including the rise of disability as an accepted part of everyday life; widespread acknowledgement of disability as a social, cultural, and political phenomenon; and the willingness of many countries, joining through the United Nations, to endorse and tackle disability as a core human rights issue. Add to this: significant changes in disability and media. In contemporary society, media is a key way we learn about, experience, contest, and are controlled in our worlds. Media is also a core way to encounter disability and a key way in which it is shaped and governed in society. Social forces change media, but, in return, media powerfully influences society, especially in the realm of disability.

In order to provide essential background and concepts to understand this two-way flow of media and disability, we set out to do two main things in this chapter. Firstly, we provide a brief overview of critical disability studies, especially to equip the reader with an understanding of the social and cultural underpinnings of disability. Readers who would like a deeper exploration of disability can consult one of the excellent introductions to disability studies and theory, such as Dan Goodley's *Disability Studies: An Interdisciplinary Introduction* (Goodley, 2011), Lennard Davis' *Disability Studies Reader* (Davis, 2013), or the *Routledge Handbook of Disability Studies* (Watson, Roulstone and Thomas, 2012). Instead what we aim to do is to focus on the key aspects needed to approach media as an important realm of disability. Secondly, having established the importance of socio-cultural dynamics to disability, we discuss where media fits in. In particular, we discuss the emergence of media as a key concern in disability activism and disability studies – especially important because of media's central place in contemporary culture.

Dislodging the Medical Model of Disability

In Chapter 1, we observed that the notion of a social approach to disability has gained widespread support – whether in the form of the famous British 'social model of disability', or, in a more general sense, as part of the broad family of social approaches to disability. Social approaches to disability can be found in many different settings from law, policy, and education, through to social work and communication development, to health and medicine, disability services, and rehabilitation. The social approach to disability is also gaining recognition in the mainstream of health and medicine, which, as we noted, is something demonstrated by its influence in the landmark World Health Organization (WHO) *World Report on Disability* (World Health Organization, 2011).

As many scholars and activists have discussed, the social approaches to disability have their own limitations and problems. However, in many ways they offer major, transformative advances in how disability is conceived. Despite these steps forward, it is disappointing yet necessary to observe that in much of health and medicine (as well as other spheres of society) we still encounter disability framed in 'disabling' ways. In Chapter 1, we also introduced two such powerful, and often negative, ways of seeing disability: the moral model and the medical model. As Dan Goodley (2011) and a range of other scholars have noted, the moral model has its roots deep in antiquity, and it still bears its impress in very influential ideas that shape our lives and the place disability has in them. Questions of morality have considerable significance in media, yet are not often approached fully or productively (rare examples in this area include Boltanski, 1999; Silverstone, 2007; Tester, 2001; Spence et al., 2011). However, in contemporary society – and especially when it comes to media – it is the medical model that has particular prominence now, and so this needs some explanation.

What is the medical (or biomedical) model of disability? The medical model of disability focuses principally on the biological and medical causes of disability, disregarding environmental and social factors. Within the medical model, disability is imagined as an illness that has a physical cause, and hence can be cured or at least managed. It is thought that once the underlying cause is removed, the disability also disappears. Health is defined within the biomedical model as the absence of disease, illness, injury, or defect. In effect, the dominance of this kind of narrow medical approach to disability has operated as a 'deficit' model. As Simon Brisenden put it in an early critique:

> In order to understand disability as an experience, as a lived thing, we need much more than the medical 'facts', however necessary these are in determining medication. The problem comes when they determine not only the form of treatment (if treatment is appropriate), but also the form of life for the person who happens to be disabled. (Brisenden, 1986: 173)

This medical model has been criticized for locating the problem of disability within an individual's damaged body without taking into account the way environments impact on a person's ability to participate in public life. A consequence of the medical model is that people are often identified, or referred to, by their disability. Also, the contribution that social attitudes, exclusion, discrimination, poverty, or disabling systems makes to disability is ignored or downplayed.

The recognition of the inaccurate and damaging nature of the medical model of disability gathered momentum from the mid-1960s onwards. One of the most famous critiques of the medical model is a famous thought experiment. This is the fable of a village inhabited by people with disabilities, conceived by South African émigré Vic Finkelstein, one of the great disability activists and thinkers. Finkelstein postulated a village run by disabled people in wheelchairs, who create their built environment and society in their own image. In this disabled village, for instance, builders construct houses with lower roofs. The knock-on effect is that able-bodied people living in the village keep hurting their heads on the low roofs. Sadly, the able-bodied minority has to have 'special equipment' fitted by disabled doctors and experts so they are able to function in this disabled society – to accommodate these abnormal able-bodied folk to the norm of low roofs (Finkelstein, 1980).

The disabled village example shows that it is possible to reimagine and redesign society so that barriers and systems of exclusion are removed. After all – as is commonplace today – a student who is a wheelchair user can easily study at university if their lecture theatre, tutorial room, or library is accessible to them. Or someone who is Blind can now access books and journal articles, search the Web, update their status on Facebook, and write and submit essays if the digital technology vital to university life has accessible interfaces.

Finkelstein's disability village is a handy encapsulation of the core idea underpinning what became referred to as the 'social model' of disability. Developed by various British disability activists and theorists, and best elaborated in the work of Colin Barnes (Barnes and Mercer, 2010) and Michael Oliver (Oliver, 1990; Oliver and Barnes, 2012), the social model has been highly influential in shifting the mainstream understanding and approach towards disability. The social model of disability is especially helpful for emphasizing the barriers by which society disables people. However, the social model has been criticized for not coming to grips with the deeper social, cultural, bodily, and experiential dimensions of disability – revealed, for instance, in intellectual disability, illness, or mental health. Debate about the social model has raged back and forth, especially in the 1990s and 2000s (Barnes, Oliver, and Barton, 2002; Shakespeare, 2006; Oliver and Barnes, 2012). Now it is common for scholars to take a pluralistic view. There are various schools of thought that seek to capture the relationships among people's bodies, minds, selves, societies, and their environments that oppress and exclude people regarded as having disability (Siebers, 2008; Goodley, Hughes and Davis, 2012; Bolt, 2014; Swain et al., 2014).

The acid test for many scholars, especially those engaged in disability policy, practice, service provision, human rights, and activism, is why discriminatory, unjust, and exclusionary practices and structures of disability persist with such powerful consequences. Many people, including us, find it depressing and puzzling why real change in the area of disability is so slow to come, even when there is much more widespread recognition of it. Consider that disability injustice – and disablism and ableism (Campbell, 2009; Watermeyer, 2012; Goodley, 2014) – have deep political, social, economic, and psychological foundations. More than this, disability discrimination, exclusion, and inequality are still with us, because disability is deeply embedded in culture itself.

We can see the cultural dimension of disability most clearly when it comes to difference. The term 'differently-abled' has a point: it draws attention to the perception of people with disabilities as lacking ability or capacity (see, for instance, its use in Silvers, Wasserman and Mahowald, 1998). It also reminds us that what is at stake here is how we deal with difference. However, the term 'differently-abled' runs the risk of wishing away the situation of disability and difference. In many societies, people understandably wish to live longer, to be healthy, and to be able to do all they wish to – as we do ourselves! Attitudes concerning disability are ways in which we project and work out many of our fears about our mortality, and the limits of our bodies and minds. Hence the common saying 'I'd rather be dead than be disabled', something taken literally when it comes to prenatal termination of children with congenital impairments such as Down's syndrome. While important, celebration of difference is only part of the conversation. At a far more troubling level, we also need to understand how disability operates in our culture as a 'dustbin for disavowal' – in disability theorist Tom Shakespeare's evocative phrase (Shakespeare, 1994). This helps us to understand that an insult, such as 'ugly midget', communicates a great deal about the fear and projection of the person hurling it – not to mention the culture in which such invective gathers its meaning and force.

From this perspective it is evident that the meanings of disability have profound implications for our lives. This was pointed out by Peter Townsend, a sociologist and social policy expert (Walker, Sinfield and Walker, 2011), in a foreword to a pioneering 1966 collection on the stigma of disability, edited by Paul Hunt. In this piece, Towsend expressed his despair at what he decried as the distorted structure of British society:

> Achievement, productivity, vigour, health and youth are admired to an extreme. Incapacity, unproductiveness, slowness and old age are implicitly if not explicitly deplored. Such a system of values moulds and reinforces an elaborate social hierarchy. The disabled are as much the inevitable victims of this system as the young professional and managerial groups are its inevitable beneficiaries. (Townsend, 1966: 2)

For Townsend, the implications of such a fundamental imbalance were immense:

> The question that is therefore raised is not a straightforward one. It is complicated and immense. Is it possible to secure real gains for those who are disabled without calling for a reconstruction of society and schooling new attitudes in the entire population? (Townsend, 1966: 2)

Then, and now, disability plays a cardinal role in defining and enforcing what is 'normal' – something in which media plays an important role.

Early Writings on Media and Disability

From the mid-1960s through to mid-1980s onwards, we see a growing number of activists, artists, leaders, thinkers, and scholars producing important works on disability, challenging stereotypes, and opening up new ways of seeing. Much of their work was foundational and remains a rich resource for understanding disability. However, in this period there was little writing and research that explicitly and systematically engages with media and disability. It is from the mid-1980s onwards that we find specific and highly significant texts in which various theorists and activists examined the ways that disabling ideas, images, and stereotypes could be found across various kinds of media.

The need for inquiry into disability and the media was the subject of a pioneering 1985 paper by a founding figure in disability studies, US sociologist Irving Kenneth Zola. A key paper is Zola's 'Depictions of Disability – Metaphor, Message, and Medium in the Media: A Research and Political Agenda' (Zola, 1985). As the title of this paper reveals, Zola saw the media as a powerful influence in disability and society. Media was a key institution especially because of the power it wielded over people's mind, something Zola articulated in a striking way in a later paper:

The power of an institution is often reflected not in the possession of formal power but in the influence it holds in the minds of the population. Thus, after contact with medical institutions, people, both in and out of hospitals, tend to think of themselves and be thought of by others in terms of their diseases and disabilities. The first step to changing this situation is when the people themselves begin to question such images and such institutions. (Zola, 1989: 421)

The questioning, critical work Zola called for arrived quickly. In 1986, the landmark collection entitled *Images of the Disabled, Disabling Images* (Gartner and Joe, 1986) offered studies of the images of disability across various cultural forms, including media. The papers in the collection illustrated the ways disability intersected with a number of cultural forms, formats, and institutions such as literature, media, and education in relentlessly similar ways. Lauri E. Klobas' 1988 book *Disability Drama in Television and Film* (Klobas, 1988) followed, offering the first study to address television in depth. The book compiled a comprehensive archive of disability representation and again identified recurring characterizations and stereotypes and hypothesized about the negative impact these had on people with disability.

In 1992, Colin Barnes published an important study that in many ways represents the first systematic account of media and disability – especially setting out an agenda for reform. Anticipating many of the influential ideas in disability and the media that still hold sway, Barnes concluded that:

> Disabling stereotypes which medicalise, patronise, criminalise and dehumanise disabled people abound in books, films, on television, and in the press. They form the bedrock on which the attitudes towards, assumptions about and expectations of disabled people are based. They are fundamental to the discrimination and exploitation which disabled people encounter daily, and contribute significantly to their systematic exclusion from mainstream community life. It is also clear that recent attempts by some elements in the media to remedy the situation and 'normalise' disabled people will only partly resolve the problem. (Barnes, 1992: 19)

For Barnes, the solution lay in all media organizations providing necessary information and imagery which 'acknowledges and explores the complexity of the experience of disability and a disabled identity and ... facilitates the meaningful integration of all disabled people into the mainstream economic and social life of the community' (Barnes, 1992). To this end, Barnes offered a set of recommendations organized around representation, training, a consultative body ('to which television companies, newspapers, and advertisers can come for advice'), and a code of ethics concerning the portrayal of disabled people in the media. For instance, Barnes advised that

> corporate ignorance about disability can only be reduced if disabled people are integrated at all levels into media organisations. Since those who experience disability daily have little or no say in how they are presented on television or in the press, broadcasters, newspapers and advertisers must be encouraged to recruit disabled employees. (Barnes, 1992: 19)

A sea change was certainly in the air. In the United States, a very important anthology appeared – Jack A. Nelson's *The Disabled, the Media, and the Information Age* (Nelson, 2004). Nelson's book covered images and representations of media, as well as accounts from media workplaces, discussion of journalism as a profession for people with disabilities, as well as prescient papers on technology, media, and disability. In this period, there also appeared a number of important studies of disability in relation to specific media – notably, television and cinema.

In 1992, the first comprehensive study of disability on British television was published – Guy Cumberbatch and Ralph Negrine's *Images of Disability on Television* (Cumberbatch and Negrine, 1992). Cumberbatch and Negrine's central finding was that

the portrayal of people with disabilities on British television is indeed inadequate and that those who work in television should as a consequence give more thought to the portrayal of such people. A positive effort should now be made to deal with the issues raised by the inadequate and unsatisfactory representation of a substantial section of the population. (Cumberbatch and Negrine, 1992: 2)

In the intervening 20 years, there have been very significant and important developments in disability and television. However, there has been no follow-on or counterpart book-length study on disability and television – though there have been notable reports such as Jane Sancho's British study (Sancho, 2003). Otherwise there have been very few book-length studies of disability in relation to any media form, except cinema (and the various studies of disability in literature and the arts). Later in the decade came Ann Pointon and Chris Davies' *Framed: Interrogating Disability in the Media* (Pointon and Davies, 1997), exploring various media and cultural forms including community television, cinema, disability arts, and music. However, it is fair to say that the real ferment in the field of media and disability came from other directions – including literary, cinema, and historical studies.

Perhaps because of their cultural centrality as the twentieth century unfolded, movies became an important cultural site for exploration of disability. Martin F. Norden's 1994 *Cinema of Isolation: A History of Physical Disability in the Movies* (Norden, 1994) was the first of these accounts and remains highly influential:

Anyone remotely aware of the mainstream movie industry's penchant for constructing warped social imagery should not be surprised to learn that this divisive behaviour has extended as much to the depiction of people with physical disabilities as it has to other repressed social subgroups. (Norden, 1994: 1)

Norden discerned something striking in Hollywood screen life, namely that 'most movies have tended to isolate disabled characters from their able-bodied peers as well as from each other' (Norden, 1994: 1). The

British scholar and critic Paul Darke was another pioneering figure in the study of cinema and disability and also wrote important papers on media and disability more broadly (Darke, 1994, 1998, 1999, 2004; http://www.outside-centre.com/darke.html). Various studies since have added substantially to our understanding of the interrelationships between cinema and disability (Smit and Enns, 2001), not least interrogating the 'problem body' we find in disability and film (Chivers and Markotić, 2010). Scholars have explored the cultural links of particular genres such as horror with disability and eugenics (Smith, 2012). Researchers have discussed disability in national cinemas such as contemporary Spanish film (Marr, 2013) or Australian cinema of the 1990s (Ellis, 2008). We have studies that discuss age and disability (Chivers, 2011; Marr, 2013), or disability and diversity in film (Ellis, 2008; Cheu, 2013; Mojk, 2013). This rich work on disability and film underscores the fact that we need to push much further in pursuit of understanding the way in which media shapes disability. Or, to put it another way, the ways in which disability is mediated.

Media Approaches to Disability

Given the ferment in the field of disability today, it is surprising that there remains a disconnection among three interrelated things: disability thinking and debates; the working of the media; and the study of media and communication. There is an impasse in thinking about and, indeed, portraying media and disability evident in some of the touchstones or orthodoxies that emerged by the mid-to-late 1990s.

One such talisman is the popularity of disability guidelines in journalism. In response to critiques and ensuing public concern about insensitive and inaccurate reporting on disability – often guided by prejudice and lack of awareness rather than good journalism practice – disability advocates, press councils and regulators, and news organizations formulated guidelines for reporting and media representation of people with disabilities. We will discuss these at greater length in Chapter 4 when we come to news and disability, but, for the present, let us observe that, while formulated with good intentions and knowledge of media industries, too often the guidelines were applied mechanistically, if they were observed at all.

Another classic response to disability and media is the desire for 'positive' representations – inclusion of and affirmation of people with disabilities across media, to balance and counteract the overwhelmingly negative portrayals. This kind of desire for affirmative portrayal of disability is entirely understandable, and indeed vital. It rallies supporters of positive stories of disability against the histories and contemporary realities of people with disabilities having performed the function of a 'bad' object in society. Here media have played a highly problematic role in communicating that disability is a parlous condition to be feared, misunderstood, maligned, and, all too often, abused and reacted to with violence. While acknowledging the negative role that media continue to play in the depiction of disability, there is an obvious and real difficulty with exhorting, and largely only accepting, positive stories of disability. Even if such 'good news' stories of disability were possible, it can be argued that such simplistically affirmative accounts are ultimately untruthful, distorting, and unsustainable. By way of comparison, consider, for instance, the debates over positive representation from the revisionist attempts of other groups, notably feminists' interventions into media, or the bodies of research and practice from a wide range of other marginalized, oppressed, or minority groups, not least racialized and sexual minorities.

A good example of this impasse in disability and media can be found in the controversial case of the Australian filmmaker Michael Noonan, who, for his doctoral thesis project, sought to make a film initially entitled *Laughing at the Disabled*. In collaboration with actors with intellectual disabilities, and the disability service provider that supported them, Noonan's idea was to make fun of disability stereotypes through humour. An ensuing controversy saw the project renamed *Laughing with the Disabled* and ultimately issued as *Downunder Mystery Tour* (Noonan, 2012). Following widespread media coverage, a wide range of disability advocacy groups, disability leaders, and people with disabilities internationally critiqued and protested his project (mostly without seeing it). For those who objected to *Laughing at/with the Disabled* felt that it relied on an offensive stereotype of people with intellectual disability. In particular, it was a clear instance of someone without disability making a film about people with disability, with inadequate input and little accountability (Goggin, 2010).

The *Laughing at/with the Disabled* case is still hotly debated, but there are a number of other instances where media produced by journalists, writers, artists, and others identifying as disabled were questioned for negative, inappropriate, or offensive representations of disability. For us, the upshot of these different controversies is that they show that the push for 'positive' portrayals – what might be elsewhere, and problematically, termed 'politically correct' versions of disability – has real limits. Instead, we would point to approaches and resources from other settings, rather than counterposing 'negative' portrayals with their 'positive' flipsides. So, from disability arts, for instance, we would point to the importance of encouraging artistic experiment, cultural innovation, and a wide range of stories. From narrative approaches, oral and community histories, and recent developments such as digital storytelling, we would point to the necessity and power of acknowledging each person and particular communities' own stories. With disability central to artistic portrayal, these representations serve as an archive for changing social attitudes about disability. Yet, as Mitchell and Snyder argue regarding the necessity of representation and its discontents:

> [R]epresentation inevitably spawns discontent. All portrayal (artistic or documentary) proves potentially allegorical in the sense that the act of characterisation encourages readers or viewers to search for a larger concept, experience, or population. Thus, the effort to represent is inevitably fraught with politics. The question of disability's service to 'negative' portrayals is profoundly complex... What one generation of interpreters views as 'humane' can be challenged by the next and so on and so forth. (Mitchell and Snyder, 2000: 40–41)

Recognizing and engaging in pitfalls of representation is a vitally important task for students, researchers, consumers, and producers of media alike, especially because it requires us to move beyond simple binaries of 'good' versus 'bad' images of disability. At another level also, acknowledging the complex action of representation takes us deeper into the heartland of contemporary disability– its location, reproduction, and transformation in culture.

Disability's Role in Culture

A central problem for our knowledge of disability and the media remains the lack of understanding of culture, its dynamics, and functions. The importance of culture for accounts of disability has been on the agenda for sometime. Over two decades ago, for instance, Tom Shakespeare offered a critique of materialist (or Marxist) approaches to disability and their emphasis on societal structures, arguing that an effect of this had been to bracket out 'questions of culture, representation and meaning' that he felt social psychology and anthropology stood to elucidate. (Shakespeare, 1994: 283). Shakespeare contended that the neglect of cultural representations was bound up with a lack of attention to impairment, its specificity, and individual experience, as well as differences:

The Social Model needs to be reconceptualized: people with impairment are disabled, not just by material discrimination, but also by prejudice. This prejudice is not just interpersonal, it is also implicit in cultural representation, in language and in socialization. (Shakespeare, 1994: 296)

Shakespeare was one of the most prominent of many scholars who raised the issue of culture. The 1995 collection *Disability and Culture* was produced by two anthropologists who had worked on rehabilitation and impairment internationally (Ingstad and Whyte, 1995). Anthropology has long been a discipline for which culture and language is an indispensable starting point, and this volume is an important exploration of disability and culture across various cultures – and one in which media is also acknowledged a number of times (Ingstad and Whyte, 1995). However, it is in the pioneering work of Faye Ginsburg that media and disability has received its richest treatment thus far (Rapp and Ginsburg, 2001; Ginsburg, 2012; Ginsburg and Rapp, 2013). In the field of sociology, a 2000 collection opened up important perspectives on the question of disability and culture. Here, Sheila Riddell and Nick Watson argued for the political relevance of culture, noting that culture is 'both a source of oppression and liberation for disabled people, and is therefore central to the politics of disability' (Riddell and Watson, 2000: 1).

In the latter part of the 1990s and into the 2000s, scholars engaged with a range of ways to explore and conceptualize the cultural dimensions of disability. These include Mairian Corker (1996, 1998) who drew on feminist approaches and increasingly structuralist and post-structuralist theories (Corker and Shakespeare, 2002) to rethink disability. Scholars have also drawn attention to the importance of discourse (Fulcher, 1989; Shildrick, 2009) and other new forms of power – such as governmentality (Tremain, 2005), for instance – in shaping contemporary disability. The rise of disability studies in North America, in particular, saw a move of important research and theory across the humanities disciplines and was prominently led by literary scholars and historians. This yielded a wave of important historically attuned theorizations of culture that have reshaped disability studies and provide rich resources for studying media and communications.

An important and influential example of this work can be found in the writing of US scholar Rosemarie Garland Thomson on the figure of the freak (Garland Thomson, 1996), something we touched upon briefly in Chapter 1 in our discussion of the cultural and social histories of dwarves. Garland Thomson's famous study of physical disability in American culture and literature analyses how different bodies are taken to be 'extraordinary'. To regard such bodies as extraordinary, she argues, is in effect a way of understanding what is normal, and denying or dealing with difference (Garland Thomson, 1997). Whether it be the freak show performers that Garland Thomson discusses – or the contemporary example of prevalence of people with disability as 'like this' imagery on Facebook – we can see the continuing importance of theorization of extraordinary bodies in media and culture and the ways representation 'simultaneously buttresses an embodied version of normative identity and shapes a narrative of corporeal difference that excludes those whose bodies or behaviors do not conform' (Garland Thomson, 1997: 7).

In the 1990s, in particular, social and cultural theorists were seeking to give due recognition to the place of the body in understanding material realities, especially in the wake of important work on gender, sexuality, race, and class – and the way that power and identity worked through our bodies (Mitchell and Snyder, 1997). As well as Garland Thomson's classic work, other important research has fleshed out our understanding of disability and embodiment. Garland Thomson herself has tackled the important issue of visuality and the body in her study of staring – a very obvious way that disability is received in public culture (Garland Thomson, 2009). Staring, which can be considered an *intense* form of looking, marks disability as aberrant and contributes to the positioning of power relations between those considered (non-) disabled.

As Mitchell and Snyder argue, while disability dominates cultural narratives, we lack a coherent critical framework with which to understand them. Mitchell and Snyder provided one of the first comprehensive accounts of disability and culture through their discussion of 'narrative prosthesis' – or the way, as we shall see in the discussion regarding television in Chapter 5, that narrative functions rather like the old idea of an artificial limb, as a supplement, or to prop things up (Mitchell and Snyder, 2000). Their subsequent work focused on understanding how disability is located in culture, what its characteristics are, and what role it plays (Snyder and Mitchell, 2006). A wide range of research has tackled disability in literature, art, and aesthetics (Siebers, 2010), as well as in other cultural forms such as music (Lubet, 2011; Straus, 2011), and toys (Ellis, 2010a, 2012a).

There has also emerged a new body of disability theory to which cultural theory is central, such as Fiona Kumari Campbell's *Contours of Ableism* (Campbell, 2009), which draws on critical race and post-colonialism studies; Robert McRuer's *Crip Theory*, engaging with queer theory (McRuer, 2006); Tobin Sieber's *Disability Theory* (Siebers, 2008), taking on long-standing issues of identity and rights; Dan Goodley's argument for the importance of understanding self, relationships, and ideology in the making of culture and disability, via psychoanalysis (Goodley, 2011: 123ff.); and a relatively slim if growing body of work on disability from a cultural studies' perspective (see, for instance, Diedrich, 2005; see also, since 2009, the *Journal of Literary and Cultural Disability Studies*). These theorists ask what disability (and by extension ability) is and how it is sustained through culture. Broadly, they explore the ways in which disability is created by an oppressive system that has naturalized the concept of able-bodiedness. Just as queer theory has been used to make visible the invisibility of heterosexuality, crip theory can critique the normalization of able-bodiedness to 'question the order of things, considering how and why it is constructed and naturalized; how it is embedded in complex economic, social and cultural relations; and how it might be changed' (McRuer, 2006: 2).

McRuer explains that definitions of the 'able body' include (for example, in the *Oxford English Dictionary*) phrases such as 'free from disability'. Able-bodiedness therefore depends on the ways disability is made visible. McRuer argues that this system, which is deeply embedded in culture, demands we agree that able-bodiedness is preferable. Such a framework can be seen in a recent Guinness beer advertisement where a group of men in wheelchairs play an aggressive game of basketball. Widely received as inspirational, the ad concludes with all but one of the men standing up out of the wheelchairs as the group go to the pub with a voice over explaining 'the choices we make reveal the true nature of our character'. The men in this ad, shown to be 'free from disability' by standing and walking away, are represented as having able bodies. The fact that they all walk away, except for one who remains in a wheelchair (perhaps to illustrate the 'dedication, loyalty, friendship' of his able peers) positions able-bodiedness as the foundational identity for athletic men. This compulsory able-bodiedness that pervades media and culture conceals ideologies regarding disability. Crip theory is an embrace of non-compliance and provides an opportunity to consider the historical specifics of narratives which project compulsory able-bodiedness (Davidson, 2010, for a critique see Sherry, 2013).

So far, we have been discussing the role that disability plays in the dynamics and operations of culture, and the social implications of this. Oddly enough, disability has not received the critical attention or research it should have from scholars and disciplines that take culture as their object of studies – whether literary, cultural, or media studies, or disciplines such as anthropology or sociology. Instead, the question of culture and disability has blossomed in the disability arts movement, associated with artistic and cultural productions by people with disabilities. Thus, an important body of the literary, artistic, and theatric community and other kinds of cultural practice, as well as accompanying criticism and research, has highlighted the notion of 'disability culture' (see, for example, Vasey, 2004). Simply put, this is the idea that there are distinctive cultural practices, meanings, identities, and social relations that belong to, and characterize, people with disabilities. In the strong version of this thesis, disability culture is seen as the meanings, practices, customs, aesthetics, genres, forms, and styles that correlate to – if not define – particular communities of people with disabilities, or the wider community of people with disabilities in general. In a weaker version of this thesis, we could see disability culture as a way of imagining the communities of people with disability, whether along the lines of a 'social imaginary', or Benedict Anderson's famous argument about media's role in the rise of nationalism in the 19th century (Anderson, 1983).

So, we might speak of Blind culture or Deaf culture, or the sporting cultures associated with wheelchair basketball, or Blind cricket, or sexual cultures of disability (compared to 'normal', or normate, sexualities) (McRuer and Mollow, 2012). Less well known perhaps are the cultures associated with what are otherwise regarded as impairment or medical categories – such as the emerging recognition of autistic culture. The importance of disability culture for its proponents is that it provides a space of belonging, meaning, identity, and cultural and historical heritage and social innovation. We see this great sweep of possibility emerging across many different countries, contexts, and cultural settings. There are rich examples of disability theatre, poetry (Barlett, Black and Northen, 2011), writing, dance, performance, and art. Such reimagining of culture via disability has also been generated through the efforts of scholar-practitioners in fields such as performance studies, notably Petra Kuppers (Kuppers, 2003, 2011, 2015) and Carrie Sandahl and Philip Auslander (Sandahl and Auslander, 2005). Disability culture does no more have to be set definitively as a restricted, exclusive domain than does any other kind of specific culture. Yet if supported and nurtured, it can provide a strong basis for engagement with, and genuine recognition from, broader culture – something that we will encounter in Chapter 3 when we come to disability-specific cultures of media use.

Conclusion

In this chapter, we have explored key ideas in disability for understanding where media fits in. We have discussed the debates around the social nature of disability and the important critiques provided of dominant approaches that still influence how we see disability – especially the medical model. We have traced the emergence of media as an increasingly relevant and important element of understanding disability in society. As we have outlined, study of disability and media helps us to understand the cultural dynamics and implications of why social transformation in disability remains slow to achieve. There are various ways in which we can understand the cultural dimensions of disability, but certainly in contemporary societies across the world media is a vital part of how culture is made, preserved, transmitted, contested, reproduced, and distributed. Media involves long-standing forms and formats – whether oral, ancient, visual, print media, and electronic media – as well as those media we now think of as new – such as Internet, mobile, social, and digital media.

Thus, media is a vitally critical domain of culture, where disability is located. Like other domains, there are common, shared aspects between a specific cultural domain, such as media, and the general culture. So, we can trace the relationships, borrowing, and adaptation among how disability is depicted in cinema, and how it is represented in media forms such as news, TV drama, or social media forms. Yet there is also a *specific* set of characteristics, operations, and traits that apply to a particular media form that require us to examine and analyse it carefully, and then consider how it contributes to a wider set of cultural, social, and political logics. This is something that we will explore in the remainder of this book, turning in Chapter 3 to the question of media formats, forms, and access.

3 Media's Role in Disability

At the opening of the 2010 film *The King's Speech*, the future King George VI (played by actor Colin Firth) struggles painfully to articulate his words, giving a speech via a public address system to a large, excited crowd. His Royal Highness, or 'Bertie', as he is familiarly called, has a 'speech impediment' – a stutter. Even if the severity of the stutter is overstated in the film, it blights his conversations in everyday life with his children and courtiers alike. As the likelihood grows that Bertie will one day be crowned king, so too does his terror at speaking. What makes matters worse is the new social function and power of radio broadcasting, the great new medium of the 1930s. While the film was set some 80 years ago, the dominating theme of the power of media still resonates. For the British royal family today (especially in the wake of the extraordinary celebrity of Princess Diana), effective exercise of power and authority requires a strong engagement with the media.

The King's Speech portrays a situation where there are striking cultural, political, and social issues in media and highlights how these are very much bound up with disability. Radio is the talking medium, so a broadcaster must 'find' their voice: that is, use it in accordance with the norms of the medium. A stutter can be turned into a pause for emphasis and effect, as Winston Churchill suggests to King George VI in the film. However, too much of a pause, stutter, or halting speech is felt to leave the audience rattled, unwilling to wait to listen to a voice that is different. The way King George VI speaks, and so uses radio, is simply not acceptable for a leader, let alone a hereditary monarch. So he must change to fit the media. There is no question that the media, or society, should change its modes of broadcasting and reception to expand the notion of communication. Hence the king must be 'saved' and his impediment 'cured' (or at least masked and ameliorated) by his speech pathologist, the expatriate Australian Lionel Logue (played by Geoffrey Rush). It is hard to resist an aside here about the telling politics of representation in *The King's Speech*. At the heart of the film is a fascinating and fraught alliance between two kinds of subjugated social individuals – those who suffer from speech impediments, the disabled, and colonial subjects of the realm, such as the unlettered speech pathologist. It is the irreverent colonial who is able, at his peril, to make fun of the reverence for the monarchy and who ultimately helps the man who would be king to overcome his subaltern status as disabled.

In this representation of radio's ascent to become an enduring broadcasting medium, we see the continuing paradox of media and disability. A new medium – in this case, radio – has entered the political realm and taken on new social meanings and functions. Radio offers new possibilities for communication, works hand-in-hand with new social arrangements (in this case the democratic challenges to the monarchy, in which the media are vitally important), and creates new cultural practices and possibilities. Reflecting on radio, we can note that it brings new accessibility of media for populations that may have, for instance, been excluded from print media and culture – for reasons of literacy, cultural capital, or disability. With radio, for instance, comes the advent of reading newspapers, books, magazines, and news for listeners who are Blind or 'print-handicapped'. Yet, by the same token, the listening technology of radio also brings new forms of exclusion.

How do people with hearing impairments, or who are Deaf, 'listen' to radio? And how do various people with disabilities, whom radio does not suit, themselves participate in the media, either as broadcasters, producers, programmers, or journalists, or as members of the 'active audience', with what later becomes 'talk' or 'talk-back' radio where people phone in to interact with a radio host (Scannell, 1991; Crisell, 1994; Turner, 2007; Bobbit, 2010)? How do emergent media technologies come to play a role in the management and control of the lives of people with disabilities, as Bill Kirkpatrick argues in relation to discourses on the 'shut-in' and US radio in the 1920–1930 period? (Kirkpatrick, 2012).

In this vignette of King George VI's predicament, we see how the medium of radio involved the creation and enforcing of particular norms – for instance, what is the 'normal' speech permitted in radio broadcasting. This case provides an example of the ways that media and disability relate to each other – the topic of this chapter.

We open this chapter with a discussion of the intersections between *media* and *disability*. Following this, we discuss the emergence of *specific forms of media for people with disability*. Here we consider the importance of radio and long-standing programmes and channels such as radio for the 'print handicapped' for a range of disability groups (especially Blind consumers); specific media histories linked with Braille (Blind consumers) and sign language (Deaf consumers); the emergence of captioning on television for Deaf people and those with hearing impairments; and the early emergence of computing and Internet cultures in the 1980s and 1990s, and their importance for offering media access in ways previously not possible.

In the third part of this chapter, we broaden our discussion to general questions of media and directly address the *question of access* with which the chapter has opened, still the most prevalent – and often only – way disability figures when discussed in relation to media. If media plays a more and more heightened role in society, especially in daily private and public life, how do citizens and consumers with disability *access* media? Access modes and contexts of use by the very diverse category of people with disabilities vary considerably, and we set some of these out. We explore the hopes and pitfalls of accessibility and representation through a case study of digital television, which illustrates the ways the media, especially the introduction of new media technologies, can both enable and disable.

Fourthly, we discuss how the matter of accessibility, and indeed the way it is bound up with the overarching discourse of freedom of media, has moved centre stage with the Convention on the Rights of Persons with Disability (CRPD) adopted by the General Assembly of the United Nations in December 2006. One consequence of the CRPD that is not yet widely realized is how it offers a much richer understanding of media access. Arguably, this landmark Convention expands our long-standing ideals regarding rights of freedom of expression, as well as cultural participation and citizenship that underpin accounts of media and democracy. Finally, noting the limits regarding the way media and disability is understood in policy, law, and regulation – even in a treaty as innovative as the CRPD – we suggest ways in which an appreciation of the rich complexity of disability helps us to go well beyond narrow ideas of access and accessibility, as well as conventional ideas of multimedia and digital convergence, to imagine extraordinary new possibilities for using, producing, and working with media.

How to Think with Disability in Contemporary Media

There is widespread discussion about the way in which media play an intensive, sustained, and central role in contemporary societies. This is especially the case in parts of the world where the economic centre of gravity is shifting away from agrarian, rural-based cities to either the massive urban centres regnant or emergent in the global south, or in the rise of the global trade in information and services rather than products. The media scholar Sonia Livingstone, in a much-discussed address to the 2008 International Communication Association conference, has spoken provocatively of the 'On the Mediation of Everything' (Livingstone, 2009). From inside the technological utopias of those promoting smartphones, smart television, social media, or ubiquitous computing, one leading edge of this 'mediatization of everything' certainly includes the rise and rise of digital cultures and technologies – or, more precisely, the socio-digital – in shaping and governing the conditions of our everyday lives and key domains in which we live and die, work and play, trade and consume, love and hate (Hepp and Krotz, 2014). The media has been detected on the up-and-up elsewhere also: in the influence of '24/7' news cycles; the power of new entertainment genres on television; or the possibilities that portability and affordability of media technologies, combined with digital networks, put in the hands of very many individuals around the world to make 'my media', to circulate quickly and relatively easily, through the raging torrents of media flows. So, how does this expansion of media, and its centrality in society, affect disability? If media is now, more than ever, at the heart of society, how does it interact with disability?

Media work in much different ways now than they did previously. It is often hard to sustain the claim that something is much more complex now than in previous epochs, but, if it is true, it is surely so of media. An obvious starting point is the growth in types and channels of media. In our time, public discussions of media – especially those in the business press, finance, media industries, and policy – and also among researchers and students of media – are obsessed by the multiple platforms of media, a convergence of hitherto relatively separate media forms, and what the particular appeal and market revenue is for a novel media product, service, or application. By contrast, the pioneering studies of media and disability offer us important insights into press, especially newspapers, broadcasting (television, and to a lesser extent, radio), advertising, and some other aspects of media. However, we still have very little research or useful concepts or even serviceable ideas about what we might call – after social studies of science and technology (MacKenzie and Wajcman, 1985) – the social shaping of disability in digital media. There is now a growing body of literature on disability and technology (Moser, 2000, 2006; Moser and Law, 2003; Mills, 2011a, 2011b, 2011c, 2013; Sterne and Mulvin, 2014). So questions abound, and merit inquiry and consideration.

How is disability communicated via particular platforms? What kinds of disability-specific media practices have been created or abound on video-sharing platforms, such as YouTube or Vimeo? Has the new television ecologies of Internet-enabled television, YouTube, TV apps, downloading, smart television, and digital television led to breakthroughs for producers and users with disabilities to create and circulate, and have attention paid to, their own stories and media? Does the wider public culture give any heed or weight to innovative media and cultural content and production pushing the boundaries on disability and society? Does social media introduce new forms of social participation for people with disabilities? Does it change the way audiences form and interact with content, including that concerning disability? Do the new formats in television – reality television, the turn to ordinary people featuring in media, high production value television series watched on DVD, iTunes, or downloaded – usher in new ways of seeing disability?

Much critical work in media studies has revolved around questions of representation – especially the relation of groups deemed as other, or marked out for attention, compared to those groups whose cultural centrality means they are taken for granted, or, as media students commonly learn in their introductory courses, what French critic Roland Barthes called 'ex-nomination' (Barthes, 1973). In media studies, there has been much work, for instance, on the representation of class, race, and sexuality, but scant work on the representation of disability. Much needed research and debate on the representation of disability in media is likely to tackle two interlinked hypotheses. Firstly, as we shall argue in Chapters 4 and 5, in particular, the full diversity of people with disability – not to mention the widespread incidence and implications of disability in everyday life – is not well represented in media. This amounts to a serious failure of imagination that surely would be fatal in mainstream media businesses, namely, the lack of realization that audiences include substantial numbers of people with disabilities. Secondly, as we argue in Chapter 6, people with disabilities are themselves underrepresented as producers of media, and media professionals often lack the cultural competence or training to understand disability.

Forms and Formats of Disability

In order to concretely discuss and develop these ideas about media and disability, it is helpful to understand something about the development of specific forms of media for people with disability. For many years, before media access for people with disability had become a concern of growing prominence from the 1990s onwards (as we shall shortly discuss), it was these kinds of disability-specific media forms and formats that most people had in mind when they thought about media and disability – if they thought about it at all.

Media formats for the Blind

Perhaps one of the best known media associated with disability is Braille. Devised by Louis Braille in 1824, Braille is a system of coding language in dots that can be detected by touch. Braille took some time and extended struggles to become established as a unified system, but became accepted as a standard form of reading and writing by many Blind people. By 1960 in the United States, for instance, some 50% of Blind school-aged children were estimated to be educated in, and using, Braille. Initially, Braille was associated with a distinctive form of print culture for Blind people. However, it also gave Blind people access to the wider, non-Blind world of print culture. In 1931, for instance, US President Hoover signed into law the Pratt-Smoot Act which saw the Federal government establish a coordinated library service for the Blind (Haycraft, 1962). This programme commenced with Braille books, then expanded, utilizing new technologies, to include 'Talking Books' (RCA, 1937). These were books and magazines recorded on records, then, once available, tapes; the machines to play these were also on offer (Haycraft, 1962). Producing materials in Braille, however, is a lengthy process, requiring considerable expertise, and still remains relatively laborious and expensive today. These limitations were noted by P.W. Nye in 1964:

> For close on a hundred years Braille permitted the blind little more than a glimpse at the world's literature. It is true that the horizons have been slowly widening, but there are many ways in which the intelligent blind person is still severely handicapped. (Nye, 1964: 247)

Expressing hopes for the development of automated reading machines, Nye judged that 'it would be eccentric to suggest that portable reading machines will never be made available to individual blind people, although it is true to say that this prospect is a very long way off' (Nye, 1964: 262).

From the 1920s, radio began to be widely used as a way to provide news, information, and entertainment to Blind listeners, or those with vision impairment, or others who, for a range of reasons, were unable to access printed material. Internationally, the idea of a radio reading service for the Blind appears to have developed in the late 1960s, with the first service established in the United States in 1969, the Minnesota Talking Books Network. The Association of Radio Reading Services was established in 1977 and is now the International Association of Audio Information Services (IAAIS) with a mission to support 'audio information services that provide access to printed information for individuals who cannot read conventional print because of blindness or any other visual, physical or learning disability' (http://iaais.org/).

In Australia, for instance, a 'special radio communications service for the blind and other people with reading difficulties' was allocated funding and spectrum by the Federal government in 1978 (Commonwealth of Australia, 2010). In Australia, such users were termed 'print handicapped' and were estimated to number nearly 20% of the population. However, as well as those more conventionally regarded as having a 'disability', such as Blind people or people with vision impairments, 'print handicapped' includes people with low literacy levels. The term is an interesting one because, unintentionally perhaps, it highlights the way in which each medium sees some potential users as 'handicapped' or excluded. Radio reading services are still an active and important element of disability media. AMI-audio, the Canadian national service, describes itself as

> the world's largest broadcast reading service making local, national and international news and information accessible. Daily, our volunteers read and record current articles from leading newspapers and magazines, which are broadcast on TV and online into more than 10 million Canadians homes. (AMI-audio, 2012)

Radio reading typically involves sufficiently sighted people to read material, as well as produce programmes, and manage media organizations. Before radio's convergence with the Internet, radio reading services had various limitations, not least the 'general disadvantage of requiring its listeners to wait for information to come to them' (Williamson, Schauder and Bow, 2000).

However, because radio is an audio medium, it offers much greater opportunities for Blind people to make their own media. With the advent of digital technologies, especially computers, accessible software tools, and the Internet, radio became a medium of tremendous innovation for Blind people. However, there is also a long history to Blind people's involvement in radio broadcasting, especially community broadcasting. For example, the *British Wireless for the Blind*, which provides audio equipment customized for use by people with vision impairment, was established in 1929 by Captain Sir Beachcroft Towse, who lost his sight in 1900 during service in the Boer War. With the advent of the technical capability to transfer audio files via the Internet, especially with the invention of the World Wide Web, it became possible to stream audio – this saw a proliferation of broadcasting radio to individual users. Such radio broadcasting typically did not require a licence, so it was entirely possible for technically adept radiophiles to set up programmes and channels, in the tradition of 'ham' and amateur radio broadcasting. Blind users realized the potential of this new Internet radio medium relatively early on, and established services such as reading from newspapers and books as well as entertainment programmes.

The development of formats and technology for Blind users has rich links with general histories of reading machines (Mills, 2013) that is now of great significance in the present media transformations. The iconic Braille system, and its associated media, is now in decline, displaced by other kinds of technology Blind people now favour. The rise of such digital technologies – particularly screen reading and other software, as well as associated devices, in which Blind people have often been early adopters and innovators – has meant that there is less incentive to use Braille, as a wider world of media and culture has now opened up. The ability to manipulate digital content is particularly useful to people with disability (Ellis and Kent, 2011: 148). The place of the Internet in such digital encoding of information adds further dimensions to its possibilities (Ellis and Kent, 2011: 148).

Many people have seen the advent of digital technologies, especially with the realm of the Internet, as a utopia. As Ellis and Kent (2011) suggest, there are many visions of digital utopia. Disappointingly, as we have already seen, the reality – even with the much more potentially flexible, configurable software, hardware, systems, and applications that make up online media – is that accessibility is still often viewed as too complicated (Ellcessor, 2014; Blanck, 2015). This is especially the case if there is a perception that accessibility will impact on the web experience of non-disabled users. Our argument, contrary to this de facto, status quo view, is that, given the opportunity, training, and resources, most web users are likely to embrace flexibility and seek to individualize their web experience through a number of available options. Just as people without disability seek to individualize their web experience through software and hardware, for people with disability this individual flexibility may include 'speech synthesis programs, vocalization programs, custom pointers, Braille displays, or portable devices designed for blind people on the go' (Kuusisto, 2007).

We can see this creative appropriation and domestication of Internet technologies, and the dialectic of accessibility working through, in the case of radio. Accessible Internet platforms that open up new paradigms of media circulation, exchange, and audience response have led to the development of other media such as radio to be made more available to communities of people with disability. Radio really arrived as a widespread, convergent, Internet form with the take-up of podcasting. Podcasting saw a form of on-demand radio, where radio stations and broadcasters would make programmes available for download at the listeners' convenience, to be played on portable digital music and audio devices, or mobile phones, rather than traditional radio receivers. Again, Blind broadcasters were in the vanguard of podcasting as a culture of use, and inflected podcasting with their own particularities of usage.

Media formats for the Deaf

There are various other media associated with other disability communities that have generated distinctive cultures of use. Deaf people share the common heritage of sign language, which has given rise to distinctive visual and tactile forms of symbol, culture, art, and communication (Nomeland and Nomeland, 2012), and, as evident in sign language literature (Bauman et al., 2006), Deaf theatre (Baldwin, 1993), or other forms of Deaf culture. While sign language is regarded as the native language and central to the identity of capital 'D' Deaf people, other languages have also been important to Deaf communities. Through a range of methods, Deaf people learn languages in order to be able to 'lip-read', as well as read and write. Yet the great shaping battle of Deaf communities and their oppression – which many term colonialization – by non-Deaf people revolves around 'oralism'.

Oralism is the doctrine that held sway from the mid-19th century until the 1970s and 1980s. Proponents believed in proscribing the use of sign language in favour of teaching Deaf people to understand languages via lip-reading and writing. The measures taken to discourage and ban Deaf people from learning and using sign languages are all too reminiscent of the approaches taken by European colonizers, or majority population groups, forbidding the use of vernacular languages of those they subjected. For many Deaf people still, the difficulties they face in learning other spoken languages means that literacy levels are low compared to their non-Deaf, 'hearing' counterparts. Nonetheless, the ability of Deaf people to write and read in these non-sign languages meant that print culture provided important media for their communities. One celebrated example is of the *Silent Worker* newspaper, published by the New Jersey School of the Deaf from 1890 to 1929. Despite the firing of its celebrated editor, George Porter, the *Silent Worker* was regarded as the premier newspaper in the US Deaf community (Buchanan, 1999). As Haller notes, one main reason that such Deaf newspapers existed is because Deaf men were trained as printers from the 1900s onwards (Haller, 1993).

While print media played an important, if deeply ambiguous role in Deaf culture, electronic media such as television offer the possibility of programmes featuring presenters, audience members, and actors using sign language. Indeed, in his study of Deaf people and British television, Paddy Ladd makes the point that sign language is difficult to represent in writing or via radio. Further, that sign languages are 'highly suited to a visual medium', and therefore the 'media of film and television are even more crucial for sign communities' development than for other minority languages' (who might have some call upon electronic media for their cultural and linguistic maintenance) (Ladd, 2007: 234). Yet even in our time this rarely occurs. Potentially, sign language interpreters can translate television programmes. Yet a lack of skilled interpreters and high costs (as well as other factors such as practicality) have long tended to preclude this option. A 2003 discussion on Deaf exclusion from television in Romania and Hungary, for instance, noted that sign language interpreters were 'rarely used, even by the national public television channels... only weekly special disability programs are regularly translated into sign language' (Flora, 2003). This was the case elsewhere, as Ladd points out:

> There is little written evidence in English speaking countries of the use of sign languages on television prior to the 1950s ... Deaf/sign broadcasting on commercial stations has, with one exception, been virtually non-existent. (Ladd, 2007: 239)

This exception was adult education programmes, produced from the 1970s onwards, which saw some British sign language in schools programmes and a token use in regional news and sporadic programme interpreting. Since this time, it is more common around the world to see sign language interpreters included in broadcasts, especially in emergency communications or important national events. This bears out the point of the 'profound symbolic significance of the sign language interpreter's presence on the screen during main broadcasting programs', which, as well as providing translation for Deaf people, stands to 'educate the public about difference, equality in difference and the necessity to offer public recognition and equality dignity for people who suffer from disadvantages due to their special characteristics/disabilities' (Flora, 2003: 270).

In the absence of sign language or interpreting on television, captioning provides a way to follow a television programme for people with hearing impairments, in particular. The differing histories of captioning in the United States and the United Kingdom provide a fascinating example of the ways people with disability receive greater access to media. While the provision of captions in the United States was a result of grassroots activity by people with hearing impairments, in the United Kingdom it was a result of government legislation and market forces.

Given the difficulties faced by Deaf people in accessing television, when a movement emerged in the United States in the 1970s to advocate for access and representation, it also included demands for captioning of programmes. Captioned episodes of Julia Childs' *The French Chef* were aired in 1972 as part of a publically funded trial of captioning on television. When a Los Angeles PBS station (KCET) refused to air the programme, the Greater Los Angeles Council on Deafness (GLAD) picketed the station until the decision was reversed. GLAD adroitly marshalled the 1934 Communications Act in conjunction with the Rehabilitation Act (introduced in 1973) to take the station to the Supreme Court (Downey, 2007).

By comparison, in the United Kingdom captioning (or Teletext) was marketed to all audiences – it would provide content including 'news, sports results, stock market prices and the weather' (Schlesinger, 1985). The system became popular in the United Kingdom during the 1980s because of government involvement (p. 475). However, unlike the mandatory captioning requirements being sought in the United States, the UK government turned their attention towards creating a market by cutting the deposit required for a Teletext TV to half that of a non-Teletext set (Schlesinger, 1985: 475).

In addition to making television more legible for many Deaf people, the provision of text descriptions of programmes on screen also provided a form of access for people with hearing impairments. Many of these people are 'post-linguistically deaf': they have experienced partial or profound hearing loss after their first experience of language as a hearing person (rather than their first language being sign language) and are usually not fluent in sign language (indeed often they have no knowledge at all). Of course, captioning is now becoming more common as a way for anyone with capacity to read and understand written language to follow television in noisy or acoustically difficult environments, such as aeroplanes or public places such as bars. It should be noted, of course, that there is a small though significant group of hearing children of Deaf parents – including the renowned disability scholar Lennard Davis (Davis, 2000).

Media: A Question of Access

The discussion of specific forms and formats inevitably highlights the threshold issue in media and disability: access. Without access to a form of media, a person is excluded from the experience that follows and is enjoyed by others. This is dramatized, for instance, in the common case of interesting and important films about disability that are all too often premiered or screened in inaccessible movie theatres. Or the frustrating experience of watching a television show without being able to follow the sound, and so losing a key aspect of dialogue, soundscape, and music, which are important to the meaning and rituals of television. Here we offer a thumbnail sketch of some key dimensions of access to media by people with disabilities. From the outset, it is important to establish that access, like other aspects of media and disability outlined above, is far from a straightforward thing.

Media access for people with disability came into stark relief with the privatization and deregulation of media industries from the 1980s onwards. Approaches to media access for people with disability had varied greatly, but there appears to have been little systematic effort to gain a comprehensive picture, let alone gather meaningful data or statistics. With the introduction of new technologies and changes in media policy, access for people with disabilities to media – especially in the electronic media (broadcasting) and new digital media (telecommunications, Internet) – becomes a widely debated, recognizable issue. In telecommunications, there had been the concept of universal service (originating in the United States), which was broadened during the course of the 1990s in many countries, to formally include access to telecommunications services for all regardless of disability. A milestone in discussion of access occurred with the 2003 European Congress on Media and Disability, and its accompanying Declaration (European Congress, 2003). By 2015, many countries have articulated clear policies on media access and inclusion that address key issues for people with disabilities – at least in digital, convergent media. Despite this, there remains little research and data available on media access for people with disabilities (see, for instance, Ofcom, 2011).

Digital television offers a handy example of these contradictions of accessibility, illustrating the ways the media – especially via the introduction of new media technologies – can simultaneously enable and disable. Digital television offers improved picture and sound quality as well as more content than analogue television. It can be distinguished from the analogue terrestrial system through 'the amount of information it can deliver and the flexibility that broadcasters have to manipulate the form in which that information is presented to the viewer' (Weber and Evans, 2002: 437). The capability to manipulate the form in which information is presented to the viewer offers significant potential to people with disability who may experience difficulty in watching television due to the effects of their impairments.

Slater, Lindström, and Astbrink (2010) identify several areas where people with disabilities could benefit from digital television, including audio description, signing subtitles, spoken subtitles, and clean audio provision. People who are Deaf or hard of hearing are frequently touted as a group who could greatly benefit from the affordances of digital TV through captions. Other methods of translation and description benefit a sizeable portion of the disability community, including people who predominately communicate in sign language, people with both hearing and vision impairments, and people with dexterity impairments (Pedlow, 2008).

As the switch to digital television has taken place in a number of countries, we have some understanding now of what people with disabilities need in order to access digital television in ways that they were excluded from analogue. One Spanish study offers important insights into the basic accessibility requirements that people with disabilities need to access digital TV. According to Utray et al., people with hearing impairments require the following accessibility features to access television:

(i) subtitles available for 100% of the broadcast content;
(ii) the use of sign language in newscasts, documentaries, and education programmes;
(iii) a clean audio service available for dramatic or fictional contents (Utray et al., 2012).

They outline other ways in which people with vision impairments and physical disabilities could benefit from accessibility available via digital television:

> The audio description service is essential for fiction programmes and documentaries. However, this group also requires that interactive services, such as the electronic program guide (EPG), be accessible by means of audio navigation systems... People with residual vision also require enhanced graphical user interfaces. People with physical disabilities have also defined their user requirements for television, focusing on the need for interactive navigation systems and the ergonomics of hardware and software to be adapted to the great heterogeneity of their needs (p. 2).

Utray et al. (2012) suggest:

> The elderly and people with intellectual disabilities can benefit from applications that address any of the requirements mentioned above, provided these applications follow a 'design for all' strategy... This approach postulates that if products and environments are designed and developed taking into consideration the demands of people with special needs, all users can benefit from the usability and quality of these products (p. 2).

While theoretically these should be available via digital channels or online, the experience of the digital transition process shows a different picture. For example, an audio description technical trial was conducted by the Australian government on the public broadcaster the ABC during 2012. Despite receiving favourable consumer feedback from people with vision impairment who claimed to experience social inclusion for the first time (Henley, 2012), rather than continue funding for the service or mandate AD requirements, the government announced another trial on catch up television three years later. While audio description may not currently exist on Australian television, various legal mandates have seen an increasing provision of this service in the United Kingdom and the United States (see Alper et al. 2015), with some UK broadcasters achieving up to 100% audio described content 6 months after legislation was put in place requiring only 10% (Ofcom, 2013). A 2013 report by the European Commission addressed the evolution of e-accessibility in relation to television and found that accessibility is more widely available on digital and online television in countries where legislation requiring audio description services is in place (Kubitschke et al., 2013).

While a number of commentators (Goggin and Newell, 2003a; Ellis, 2012b, 2014; Jaeger, 2012) identified digital television as a key site of potential social inclusion and exclusion for people with disability, television is developing at a rapid pace and can now mean any video enabled screen. Captioning again emerged as significant disability media concern in the development of television's transition to the Internet. When Netflix sought to publicize their service through a free screening of *The Wizard of Oz* in celebration of the film's 70th anniversary, Deaf activists launched a campaign against the video streaming service. Captioned versions of the film are widely available through both DVD and broadcast release. While Netflix cited technological difficulties in streaming captions through their software (Microsoft Silverlight), for many viewers with hearing impairment the oversight represented another instance where they were not taken seriously as audiences or customers (for a full discussion, see Ellcessor, 2012). Just as they had in the 1970s, a number of Deaf activists, this time led by the National Association of the Deaf (NAD) and the Western Massachusetts Association of the Deaf and Hearing Impaired, took Netflix to court under the Americans with Disabilities Act (ADA). Netflix attempted to argue that as an online space it was not subject to the same accessibility requirements as physical spaces such as the Cineplex. However, the courts disagreed and Netflix was ordered to

> maintain on its website (www.netflix.com) a list or similar identification of On-demand Streaming Content with Conforming Captions and Subtitles...Netflix's obligation to maintain this list will expire on October 1, 2014, by which point Conforming Captions or Subtitles will be available on 100% of On-demand Streaming Content. (Wolford, 2012)

The NAD responded favourably to the ruling with predictions that Netflix would become 'a model for the streaming video industry' (Mullin, 2012) as legal commentators bemoaned the impacts on video streamed online (Goldman, 2012; Sanchez, 2012).

While at the time of writing it is too early to tell whether Netflix will meet their captioning obligations, a number of other groups such as people with vision impairment seeking audio description (Joehl, 2011; Kingett, 2014) and people with hearing impairments seeking uncensored captioning (Wildman, 2013) are turning their attention towards

Netflix to advocate for an truly accessible model for the video streaming industry.

Media Accessibility, Freedom of Expression, and Cultural Citizenship

As the case of digital TV and other areas of convergent media illustrate, accessibility has become an important issue for mainstream media, governments, regulators, and the public alike. The drive for accessibility has now been further bolstered with the adoption of the UN CRPD by the UN General Assembly in December 2006. The CRPD is an epochal development in the recognition of human rights for persons with disabilities, indeed for human rights in general. What is remarkable about the Convention is the prominence accorded to recognizing the importance of media – especially new media and digital technologies – to the participation of people with disabilities in public and private life. In doing so, it not only represents a long overdue recognition of this aspect of citizenship and social inclusion for people with disabilities, it actually recasts and deepens our very understanding of the importance of media to the lives of us all.

To provide some historical perspective, consider the 1948 Universal Declaration of Human Rights. The Declaration contains the evocative, classic evocation of media's role in freedom of expression, as contained in the resonant Article 19:

Everyone has the right to freedom of opinion and expression; this right includes freedom to hold opinions without interference and to seek, receive and impart information and ideas through any media and regardless of frontiers. (UN, 1948)

Over 60 years on from the 1948 Universal Declaration, we would see media playing an important role in the realization of the key Articles 22 and 27 of that time:

Article 22.

Everyone, as a member of society ... is entitled to realization, through national effort and international co-operation and in accordance with the organization and resources of each State, of the economic, social and cultural rights indispensable for his dignity and the free development of his personality.

Article 27.

(1) Everyone has the right freely to participate in the cultural life of the community, to enjoy the arts and to share in scientific advancement and its benefits. (UN, 1948)

Subsequently, the international community has built upon such principles with the efforts through UNESCO on the 'New World Information and Communication Order' (MacBride, 1980), the International Telecommunications Union's work on telecommunications and development, and, most recently, in the 2005 World Summit on the Information Society (Raboy and Landry, 2005; Servaes and Carpentier, 2006). Communication and media scholars and activists have also theorized and debated the nature of communication and cultural citizenship rights (Dakroury, Eid, and Kamalipour, 2009; Padovani and Calabrese, 2014), including the notion of such rights including disability (Hoffman and Dakroury, 2013; Goggin, 2015).

The existing international treaty framework, the domestic human rights and anti-discrimination law and policy arrangements, as well as the existing norms and practice regarding technology, have led to a very slow, indeed at times hostile and difficult, process for people with disabilities wishing to exercise their rights to social, economic, cultural, and other participation through digital technology (Goggin and Newell, 2003a). There are notable achievements worldwide in access, inclusion, and design by people with disabilities in technology – especially from the application of various national general anti-discrimination laws such as, in the anglophone world, the 1990 US Americans with Disabilities Act, the Australian 1992 Disability Discrimination Act, and the 1995 UK Disability Discrimination Act, as well as other specific laws, regulations, and social policy – but puzzling gaps and most regrettable exclusions remain, as we have noted (Goggin and Newell, 2003a). This is curious given the 1990s was the period when the Internet's diffusion sharply increased around the world, and when mobile phones became commonplace, and yet people with disabilities had to fight many battles for belated and poor access (Goggin and Newell, 2003a).

Against this history, it is noteworthy indeed that among the general obligations of the Convention set out in Article 4 are unprecedented and powerful requirements for states to pursue research and development of universal design, and of new technology (especially with reference to affordability), and to provide accessible information to people with disabilities concerning a range of mobility aids, devices, and technologies (Articles 4, 9, CRPD). Perhaps the most significant new article in the CRPD is Article 21, which clearly extends the famous Article 10 of the 1948 Declaration address to people with disabilities by emphasizing the importance of accessible media and communications:

> States Parties shall take all appropriate measures to ensure that persons with disabilities can exercise the right to freedom of expression and opinion, including the freedom to seek, receive and impart information and ideas on an equal basis with others and through all forms of communication of their choice . . . including by:

> a) Providing information intended for the general public to persons with disabilities in accessible formats and technologies appropriate to different kinds of disabilities in a timely manner and without additional cost . . . ;

> d) Encouraging the mass media, including providers of information through the Internet, to make their services accessible to persons with disabilities;

> e) Recognizing and promoting the use of sign languages. (Article 21, CRPD)

In doing so, Article 21 of the CRPD creates as yet undiscussed possibilities for how we understand media and freedom of expression in general.

Future Possibilities: Rethinking Access

Accessibility has been brought to centre stage by the new CRPD, with greater dimensions of accessibility and design being made an integral part of international human rights as they relate to communication and media. However, the CRPD has its own limitations, not least deriving from the negotiated nature of the treaty formed from the different positions and aspiration of the various nations involved. The CRPD also suffers from the limitations of conventional human rights, even as they now expand to properly cover disability. There are many aspects of disability, creativity, culture, what it is to be human, as well as the nature of communication, that are not well captured in our existing notion of rights. In this penultimate section of this chapter, we will explore this further, as we suggest the need for a fundamental rethinking of access and design.

With the stereotypical wheelchair user in mind, in many discussions there is a tendency to think of access issues on the model of the 'curb cut'. That is, the modification of the curbside or gutter of a road to make the pavement, and crossing of roads, in urban environments especially, navigable by wheelchair and scooter users, and other pedestrians with mobility technologies and aids. Yet this kind of common form of design and modification in the built environment, hard-won though it is, is simply one facet of a complex picture of access. A good definition is provided by Canadian disability studies scholar Tanya Titchkovsky, who regards access as a 'way that people have of relating to the ways they are embodied as being in the particular places where they find themselves' (Titchkovsky, 2011: 3). Titchkovsky argues:

> Access, then, is tied to the social organization of participation, even to belonging. Access not only needs to be sought out and fought for, legally secured, physically measured, and politically protected, it also needs to be understood – as a complex form of perception that organizes socio-political relations between people in social space. (Titchkovsky, 2011: 4)

Titchkovsky writes about her own university, as well as the difficulties faced in gaining acceptance for the importance of access as a general issue – something that, for university students and teachers reading this book, also applies to us.

Titchkovsky notes that once we become aware of the concept of disability, we often divide our world into people who need access (and may or may not have it), and people who do not. Titchkovsky urges us to fundamentally question this taken-for-granted approach on access, suggesting that this naturalizes the kinds of exclusion and inclusion that exist in spaces and places such as our educational institutions. Rather, she contends that, as well as generating 'demands' for more access, or better accessibility, we also need to fundamentally see access as about the normative structure of space, social relations, and action for all of us (Titchkovsky, 2011). While this notion of access might seem difficult to get hold of, it is important especially for thinking about media, where the question of access is often confounding rather than straightforward.

Take the case of the accepted method by which video, television, and film are made accessible to Blind audiences or users. As we have discussed, this is called 'audio description' and involves devising and recording an audio track that accompanies the moving image (and visual dimension) and can be listened to by the Blind viewer. Audio description provides additional aural information about what is occur-ring in screen. It has taken considerable struggles to have the right for audio description to be taken as a normal part of broadcast media, film, and video. It is an easier process, in many ways, with DVD, digital tele-vision, and even computer devices, where more information and tracks can be provided with a programme, and indeed often are, for instance, interviews, out-takes, information on the production, and so on. Yet the process of making audio description is much more complex than it might seem. It involves the production of an authorized description, or 'reading' of what a visual medium conveys; it therefore needs to con-sider what meanings or aspects are important for a viewer, and thus what should be described in the audio track. While there are protocols and norms, shared expectations about how audio description should be done, and professionals who specialize in this, nonetheless the complex questions of how we should translate media across the senses are pro-found indeed. Our current approaches to access, in one sense, represent particular ways to achieve this.

In seeking to open up creative approaches, especially through art and performance, a 2012 workshop at the University of Michigan saw par-ticipants exploring 'cross-sensory translation'. In her lecture, disability scholar Susan Schweik drew parallels between the kind of description that disability often seems to require or call up, and *ekphrasis*, tradition-ally understood in literary traditions as the textual description of a visual work (Schweik, 2012; for another such project, see Kudlick and Schweik, 2014). This idea reminds us of the tradition of thinking and enacting translations across visual, verbal, and plastic media – between paint-ing and the written word, for instance, or music and architecture. All of us are engaged in and can explore translation across the senses, and thus creative approaches can move us well beyond restricted accounts of access to media that are based on narrow ideas about people and 'disability'.

Conclusion

This chapter has offered an overview of the intersections between dis-ability and media from issues of access, representation, and legislation to specific media forms such as Braille, Blind radio and television caption-ing. We have also introduced the significance of the emerging digital environment as a continuation of older media, replete with the ability to both enable and disable.

While we have sought to draw parallels with other subjugated groups and their relationship with the media, the issue of disability is unique and has not been adequately dealt with within disability nor media studies, nor the health sciences. What this impasse reveals, in our view, is that our concepts of what both disability and media are, are outdated, limited, and inaccurate.

Starting with disability, we note that the best research, thinking, cultural production, and media practice suggests that we are still at the early stages of understanding what exactly the social constitution of disability is. That is, disability is a vastly richer and more complex social phenomenon and experience than previously thought. Further, as we appreciate and seek to understand the new social coordinates of disability, it leads us, in turn, to seek a better explanation of society, and the operation and nature of the social. That is to say that disability is actually central to how society is conceived and operates, how it is structured, and how its circuits and networks connect us into a society. This places disability at the frontiers of social theory.

Turning to media, we are commencing from even further back when it comes to disability, as we have briefly suggested. Compared to particular ventures or sub-fields of research such as feminist media studies, sexuality and media, post-colonialism and media, race and media, or migration, diasporas, and media, disability and media is barely a shoal in a now fast-expanding archipelago of dedicated specialisms in media and communication studies. For instance, disability and communication (or media) is significantly overshadowed and outranked in prestigious journals and research in comparison with health communications. Yet there is great ferment and intellectual excitement in media and communications studies. From this are emerging important conceptual advances and theories about the transformations in media, and how these are tightly interwoven with transformations in the social. So, in our minds, an obvious direction for those interested in disability and media, and building an adequate theory, is joining these still two separated and distinctive theoretical projects.

4 The News on Disability

News headlines encapsulate many of society's dominant attitudes, and disability is no exception. Take this following collection of headlines:

> The boy who never gave up: Inspirational story of how paralysed rugby player overcame his disabilities to win job at top legal firm. (Levy, 2009)

> Disabled veteran does the impossible: A former paratrooper was told he would never walk again. He didn't listen. (Springer, 2012)

> Inspirational disabled children, YouTube Video playlist (YouTube, 2013)

> Farsighted engineer invents bionic eye to help the blind. (Lin, 2013)

> Fraudulent disability claims threatening social security program: $21b in false disability claims. (Wiser, 2013)

> Franklin county woman accused of taking $20,000 from disabled veterans. (*State Journal*, 2013)

Such news headlines are all too familiar. As we have discovered, there are particular and peculiar ways in which people with disabilities figure in the media – as subjects of media coverage and discussion, media audiences, consumers, or users. In this chapter, we will look at how media portray and represent disability, and people with disabilities, in a key form of media – news. Underlying our discussion is the argument that when it comes to media, representation still matters very much. This is true of disability, as much as social categories that have received much more attention and debate, such as gender, sexuality, race, ageing and youth, and class.

A good place to understand media representation of disability – indeed, to critically take its temperature – is in the area of news. Armed with an understanding of disability in news, we can better understand, decipher, and confront stereotypes, myths, and images of disability. Through media such representations of disability have a potent influence on how we understand social identities. This is important; in the words of Graeme Innes, the former Australian Disability Commissioner:

> People with disabilities are almost inevitably depicted in the media as victims or heroes. We are neither of those. We are just people who want to be agents of our own destiny. What that does is reinforces the negative way in which society put limits on people with disability. (Graeme Innes, quoted in Burns, 2010)

In what follows, we will explore how disability figures in what is regarded as news. We will look at how reporters and journalists depict disability. We'll also consider how media workers interact with people with disabilities as sources, celebrities, and victims. Discussing perceived problems in how disability is reported, we will look at the limitations of 'guidelines' to deal with the issues raised. Then, via a case study of the 2012 London Paralympics, we'll explore the potential of creative, new approaches to representing disability through news and media.

News

News remains vital to contemporary media. Though its industrial structures, business models, and professional norms are undergoing intense transformation (Anderson, Ogola and Williams, 2014), news retains a strong social function. In classic theories of media, news lies at the heart of the media's role as a fourth estate. It provides information for citizens to follow and understand their societies, and to be able to actively participate in them. Through news, media fulfil their long-standing role as gatekeeper and watchdog. News is also closely associated with the prized undertaking of investigative journalism, where experienced journalists research and report issues of key importance in the public sphere. For all these, and other reasons, news is believed to have a significant influence on the formation of societal attitudes.

News media have their own distinctive formats, industrial organization, political economy, routines, and organizations. At a global level, we can see that news remains dominated by a handful of key companies, now typically well-known global brands (Boyd-Barrett, 2010). Reuters and AAP are the two most prominent, long-standing news agencies. In the anglophone world, CNN, Fox, and the BBC are household names, recently joined by Al-Jazeera – which, in addition to its Arabic-language channels, offers the popular Al-Jazeera English. The relatively concentrated nature of news globally has been a well-established phenomenon, part of what has been perceived internationally as a key force in cultural imperialism. Yet the visibility of these global outlets, and such accounts, can obscure the important ways in which news, its interpretation, and functions can be very much a national and local phenomenon (Boyd-Barrett and Rantanen, 1998; Sassen, 2007). Much news forms its meanings at a national level still (Jensen, 1998). Further, the sub-national, local contexts are highly significant. This is the case also in the way that local contexts in different countries knit together to work across the national – a phenomenon that scholars have called 'translocal' (Kraidy and Murphy, 2003).

Two further transformations in news are important to briefly note. Firstly, the classic account of news (and media) playing a function in a public sphere (Wodak and Koller, 2008; Gripsrud et al., 2010), where debates occur about politics and democracy has been fundamentally challenged. Theorists have argued for the importance of settings of everyday life and changed relationships between private and public spheres for understanding media (Silverstone, 2007; Coleman and Ross, 2010). These new theories offer an opportunity to make sense of the productive role of new genres of news. Many people now gain their news and current affairs through comedy and satire formats (Gray, 2008; Gray, Jones and Thompson, 2009). The relationship between information and entertainment has been reconfigured in other ways with the rise of the celebrity, of infotainment formats, and other developments (Turner, 2013; de Botton, 2014). Finally, convergent digital media has seen the rise of new kinds of news gathering, production, and distribution (Chadwick, 2013), from citizen journalism to the news for intimate publics (Berlant, 2008) distributed by individuals through social media (Papachrissi, 2010).

This brief reminder about the industrial and economic underpinnings and cultural landscapes of news is important for setting the scene for understanding how disability and news interact. For at least 30 years, there has been an interest in how disability is represented in news. The bulk of studies have investigated the representation of disability in print media, especially newspapers. By the early 2000s, such studies had convincingly shown the prevalence of stereotypes of disability in news and associated forms of media. One of the first scholars to offer a systematic account of the stereotypes used in newspapers was J. S. Clogston. Building on the work of Clogston, Beth Haller has investigated different aspects of disability and media, especially news, in many studies, culminating in her book *Representing Disability in an Ableist World* (Haller, 2010). In her early work, Haller drew upon content analysis methods; that is, systematically selecting, coding, enumerating, and analysing content from media texts to investigate how these depict disability. Such approaches allowed Haller and many other scholars to explore, in the words of one of her studies, how 'the news frames disability' (Haller, 2010). Framing theory is an area in its own right in media studies, and we won't be able to discuss it at length here. What is useful about framing theory is its central precept – evident here in Haller's proposition – that certain 'frames' of meaning shape how we approach and make sense of phenomena we encounter in the world (Entman, 1993 and 2007). News frames create context and set limits around a story by emphasizing certain things, attitudes, and personal qualities while ignoring others. As Blood, Putnis, and Pirkis (Blood, Putnis and Pirkis, 2002) explain, frames refers to the way the media 'packages' a news story. Recognizing such perceptual lens means that it is possible to think about how to reframe phenomenon (Warren and Manderson, 2013).

Applying framing theory to disability, Haller and other scholars have argued that the media uses a clearly defined set of frames to communicate disability stories and shape public opinion and agenda about disability. Haller offers the following explanation of the most common news frames, beginning first with traditional frames:

The Medical Model – Disability is presented as an illness or malfunction. Persons who are disabled are shown as dependent on health professionals for cures or maintenance.

The Social Pathology Model – People with disabilities are presented as disadvantaged and must look to the state or to society for economic support, which is considered a gift, not a right.

The Supercrip Model – The person with a disability is portrayed as deviant because of 'superhuman' feats (i.e. ocean-sailing blind man) or as 'special' because they live regular lives 'in spite of' disability (i.e. deaf high school student who plays softball).

The Business Model – People with disabilities and their issues are presented as costly to society and businesses especially. Making society accessible for disabled people is not really worth the cost and overburdens businesses, that is, accessibility is not profitable. (Haller and Zhang, 2010)

As well as these 'negative' or regressive frames, Haller also identifies a number of potentially positive or 'progressive' frames that have emerged concerning disability from the 1980s onwards:

The Minority/Civil Rights Model – People with disabilities are portrayed as members of the disability community, which has legitimate political grievances. They have civil rights that they may fight for, just like other groups. Accessibility to society is a civil right.

The Cultural Pluralism Model – People with disabilities are presented as a multi-faceted people and their disabilities do not receive undue attention. They are portrayed as people would be.

The Legal Model – The media explain that it is illegal to treat disabled people in certain ways. The Americans with Disabilities Act and other laws are presented as legal tools to halt discrimination. (Haller and Zhang, 2010)

Such 'progressive' frames are still a 'way of seeing' the world – they are a way of encoding or making sense of reality. However, for many people these new frames represent 'progress' in societal attitudes towards disability – in which new scripts and stories about disability in the media are advanced.

Take, for instance, the way in which news media framing affects how people respond to this disability. We can find a good example in the way that disability writer Riley summarizes the frames news media and talk shows use to describe the paralympian Aimee Mullins:

First there are the headlines: 'Overcoming All Hurdles' (she is not a hurdler, although she is a long jumper) or 'Running Her Own Race', 'Nothing Stops Her' or the dreaded and overused 'Profile in Courage'. Then come the clichés and stock scenes, from the prosthetist's office to the winner's podium. Many of the articles dwell on her success as the triumph of biomechanics, a 'miracle of modern medicine', turning her fairy tale into a Coppelia narrative (or *Six Million Dollar Woman* movie sequel). (Riley, 2005)

Riley's 2005 reading of the way in which Aimee Mullins is represented has much resonance today. A surprising amount of contemporary media is premised upon the assumption that what is newsworthy about disability is its inspirational character. This may come as a surprise to many readers: after all, aren't many more people now – perhaps 'everyone' – aware about the need to not be patronizing about disability? Isn't there a much wider range of representations of disability, as well as enhanced prominence of people with disability even in mainstream media? There is some truth to this. We'd agree that there is much greater awareness about attitudes and media portrayal of disability in 2014 compared to even one decade before. So, yes, in some ways, established mainstream media may be more aware that this way of seeing disability through the lens of 'inspirational' or 'uplifting' is patronizing, and extremely limiting. Yet stereotypical portrayal of disability still abounds – even in what is often regarded as cutting-edge, funky, social, and digital media.

A good example may be found in the common representation of disability among the most shared and consumed social media. Among the most popular viral videos in 2012, for instance, was a video of US veteran Arthur Boorman. The upbeat and moving video tells the story of how – after 15 years of not being able to walk, and being overweight – through the unstinting support of one particularly dedicated and motivated yoga teacher, he is able to walk again. One fan of the video praised it as follows:

> We're glad we have video of this story because it's almost impossible to believe. Arthur Boorman is a disabled Gulf War veteran. Doctors told him he would never walk again ... He lost his will to live, gained a ton of weight and thought his life was over. Then he decided to change everything ... Boorman goes from a guy who was told he'd never walk again to a guy who can sprint through the park on his own free will ... The next time you feel like complaining about your life, you may want to remember Arthur Boorman and realize that everything is up to you. (Jones, 2012)

In this popular video – and the genre of disabled veteran videos to which it belongs – disability is framed as a 'must-watch', newsworthy content, because it is inspirational and uplifting to the human spirit. This common appeal of disability as an instructive moral fable lives on, even in contemporary online social media.

So why is this a problem? It is not a good thing to have media instruct us with inspirational materials? Surely this is better than 'bad' news, or, worse still, trashy, sensational content. To understand why the disability-as-inspirational myth is a problem, consider this critique provided by the Australian *Ramp Up* disability blog journalist Stella Young:

We all learn how to use the bodies we're born with, or learn to use them in an adjusted state, whether those bodies are considered disabled or not. So that image of the kid drawing a picture with the pencil held in her mouth instead of her hand? That's just the best way for her, in her body, to do it. For her, it's normal. (Young, 2012)

Young continues:

I can't help but wonder whether the source of this strange assumption that living our lives takes some particular kind of courage is the news media, an incredibly powerful tool in shaping the way we think about disability. Most journalists seem utterly incapable of writing or talking about a person with a disability without using phrases like 'overcoming disability', 'brave', 'suffers from', 'defying the odds', 'wheelchair bound', or, my personal favourite, 'inspirational'. If we even begin to question the way we're labelled, we slide immediately to the other end of the scale and become 'bitter' and 'ungrateful.' We fail to be what people expect. (Young, 2012)

Over the top? But isn't it hard to live with disability? Isn't living a 'normal' life an achievement? Shouldn't we be sensitive enough to appreciate the 'courage' this takes?

Let us explore this disability-as-inspiration trope further by looking at the quite different ways that the news media framed stories about two different people with disabilities in Australia – paralympian athlete Kurt Fearnley compared with disability activist Sheila King. Superficially, the underlying story that is 'news' is similar in both cases. Both Fearnley and King encountered problems travelling on the budget airline Jetstar, yet were treated quite differently – by the airline and by the media.

Paralympian Kurt Fearnley is one of the best known personalities with disability in contemporary Australian society. Fearnley is variously portrayed as a national hero, a sporting legend, and as inspirational person with a disability. He is a key disability personality on the Australian media landscape, widely appreciated for his 2013 Australia Day speech in which he encouraged Australians to stop fearing people with disability. Previously, in 2012, Fearnley had appeared on *The Biggest Loser Australia* reality TV programme to inspire contestants to achieve their weight loss goals. In 2009, Fearnley used his celebrity to highlight inaccessible and humiliating air travel as an issue many people with disability face. When Fearnley was not allowed to take his own wheelchair on a Jetstar flight, he decided to crawl rather than be pushed through the airport in an 'unsuitable chair'. Some news outlets reported that he was 'forced' to crawl (Butson, 2009), without acknowledging his strength as an athlete. Fearnley declared the situation akin to an able-bodied person 'having [their] legs tied together...pants pulled down and...carried or pushed through an airport' (Butson, 2009). The story received national media attention. Critically, Fearnley's inspirational and athletic qualities lie at the heart of the framing choices made – he is a national hero, evident in the headline: 'Fearnley fury at wheelchair humiliation in airport' (Butson, 2009). The story reports Fearnley's humiliation at being asked to check his wheelchair in with his luggage at Brisbane Airport and the support he received from politicians, the human rights commissioner, and Jetstar itself after he recounted this experience at the National Disability Awards dinner.

If we analyse this episode, it is evident that mainstream media told this story through already well-established frames about disability and Fearnley's emerging persona and place in Australian society. In this story, Fearnley was largely constructed as a national hero, unnecessarily humiliated – and only seeking a better go for people with disabilities unable to stand up for themselves. In short, this episode was framed via what Haller terms the 'supercrip' model. In this processing of framing disability, light changes in phrasing will affect people's response. Consider, in contrast, the way news media portrayed disability advocate Sheila King when she attempted to sue the same airline for a similar situation.

King initiated court proceedings against Jetstar after she was excluded from a flight because two other wheelchair users had already booked the same flight. King contended that Jetstar acted in a discriminatory fashion, in its policy of only providing space for two wheelchair users on each flight. King lost her case, and for her pains received death threats. In contrast to Fearnley – who was framed as a source of inspiration seeking only to make air travel accessible to other people with disabilities – for her pains King was portrayed as an ungrateful troublemaker. If we review the news media coverage, for instance in the (former) broadsheet *The Sydney Morning Herald*, we see very interesting and significant patterns of how the event and King's subsequent complaint were represented. In particular, there is a process where competing frames are selected and 'public opinion' is represented.

As a starting point, we could see coverage of King's case depicted via the 'business model' frame, one of the underpinning assumptions of which is that disability is 'costly to society and businesses especially' (Haller and Zhang, 2010). Or we might also see the 'social pathology' frame in play, where King's quest for 'accommodation' was not presented as a right, rather something that should be conferred as a gift – for which her demand was 'unreasonable', and her protest ungrateful. As Stella Young notes, the ungrateful cripple is a familiar story that is invoked when people with disability begin questioning structural inequality. We can see this narrative surfacing in the way that comments following previous online articles are then used as primary sources of public opinion in this article. Such online comments included the following:

> Try travelling by coach
>
> Some people in wheelchairs are just plain ignorant and expect us free walking people to help them.
>
> Ms King has cost the ratepayers of this region hundreds of thousands of dollars.
>
> …am glad this woman has lost and now has to pay the costs. (Horin, 2012)

There is a telling process at play here in terms of the sources relied upon by the journalists in question. Whereas Fearnley is the main source of information in *The Age* article, online comments constitute the main source in *The Sydney Morning Herald*'s analysis of King's court loss. Fearnley's quotes underscore his inspirational qualities. By comparison, direct quotes from King are primarily used to illustrate her ungrateful attitude:

> People write things like, 'Live with it; it's not our fault you're disabled.'
>
> We've tried being nice and gentle. It didn't work. Sometimes you have to go to court. (Horin, 2012)

So, despite the broadly similar issues the two faced with barriers to airline travel, the framing of each is distinctively different. This can be also seen in the imagery that accompanied the respective articles. *The Age* article is about Fearnley competing in the Paralympics and crawling the Kokoda Trail in Papua New Guinea (a revered national site of remembrance due to its place in the Second World War battles). The image of King, by comparison, does not invoke any notions of national pride and identity. She is pictured sitting casually and comfortably in her wheelchair in the non-competitive, non-strenuous environment of her veranda in front of green palms. King is described as 'a wheelchair-bound woman' (Hall, 2012), whereas Fearnley is 'a wheelchair-marathon champion' (Butson, 2009).

Our understanding of Fearnley is bound up in notions of patriotic nationalism. His prior achievements are physical in nature whereas King's relate to costing the taxpayer more money following her previous accessibility litigation. Fearnley is an 'Aussie Battler' (a stock figure in Australian culture) giving it a go, whereas King is a whinger. Fearnley is constructed as a nice, athletic guy and King a cranky old woman repeatedly misusing the courts. Fearnley is directly quoted more often than King in these three articles and allowed, without any ado, to speak for himself and other people with disabilities. King, on the other hand, is paraphrased, leaving so-called experts – such as Nicolas Patrick, the chairman of the Redfern Legal Centre (Horin, 2012) – to be used as direct sources. This is despite King herself being an expert as both a person with disability and a disability advocate.

Thus far, we have been introducing key ideas how news media represent disability – something of which that the Fearnley and King case studies provide excellent examples. An important implication of this analysis, and the research that underpins it, is that this is not simply an issue for how we understand disability – an issue with which many may not be interested (until, perhaps, they are personally affected). Rather, we can see that disability provides particular images and metaphors, recipe or scripts, for how we understand aspects of social life or culture that actually do not have anything to do with disability (at least, not in an obvious way). So, for instance, news on scientific discovery or developments in health are often presented as newsworthy, or breaking news, because they involve a 'cure' for disability. Or people in society receive honours for their charitable works in the service of the disability community. We could take this argument one step further and suggest that how news is structured has a lot to do with disability. This is an analogous argument that is relatively well established and critiqued in relation to gender or race. Namely, that much of what is defined as 'news', or how the norms and conventions of journalism operate, are shaped by narrow ideas about gender or race. So too it can be contended with disability (though we hasten to note that a fully fledged systematic study of contemporary news and disability has not been conducted).

Framing theory and analysis is only one of a number of approaches to understanding representation of individuals and groups in news. It has been influential in disability news research, especially through the work of Clogston and Haller, as we have noted. It provides a clear way to think about the ways of seeing disability that we find in news media and journalism. There are many other potential ways to explore news imagery, structures, narratives, semiotics, discourse, and so on available in media studies which have not yet been widely drawn upon in studying disability. One of the issues we face in our responses to and analysis of disability and news are the diverse, often contradictory meanings and implications they generate. This is a key concern that has arisen with the most visible media form in this area: disability media guidelines.

Reframing the News on Disability

A strong response to the 'disabling' nature of news has not so much come from researchers as from the advocacy of disability movements. Around the world, different groups have argued that disability has not been accurately or properly represented in media, and that corrective action needed to be taken. A key strategy was the formulation of guidelines for media organizations, editors, and journalists to stipulate how disability should be covered. Charles Riley provides such 'Guidelines for Portraying People with Disabilities in the Media' as an appendix to his book *Disability and the Media* (Riley, 2005: 219ff). Over the course of at least two decades, many large organizations have devised and made available guidelines to promote greater awareness and understanding of portrayal of disability in the media. A good example is provided by the International Labour Organization (ILO), a United Nations agency, which publicizes such a set of guidelines introduced in this way:

How people with disabilities are portrayed and the frequency with which they appear in the media has an enormous impact on how they are regarded in society. Portraying people with disabilities with dignity and respect in the media can help promote more inclusive and tolerant societies and stimulate a climate of non-discrimination and equal opportunity. (ILO, 2010)

Because the ILO is a labour organization, concerned with work opportunities for all, its guidelines are intended to provide

practical advice to media on how to promote positive, inclusive images of women and men with disabilities and stimulate a climate of non-discrimination and equal opportunity for disabled persons at all levels of the economy and society. They are intended for people working as editors, journalists, broadcasters, producers, programme makers and presenters. They are also relevant to people working as web editors, and on interactive multimedia products. They reflect a commitment by the International Labour Organization (ILO) and Irish Aid Partnership Programme to promote decent and productive work for women and men with disabilities through their inclusion in programmes and services to promote their employability and employment. (LO, 2010)

While an important tool for awareness raising, the effectiveness of such guidelines has been a major issue.

In their 1999 study of disability terminology in newspaper reports in Canada and Israel, Gail Auslander and Nora Gold noted that the track record of formal guidelines on disability terminology was mixed:

Among the reasons cited for failure to adopt more sensitive terminology are lack of acceptance of the concept of 'disabling language' and agreement as to what is and is not acceptable, lack of evidence as to the outcomes of the use of disabling language, failure of publishers to specifically require the use of appropriate language, and the cumbersome nature of more sensitive phrasing. According to one scholar, style manuals, including references to disability terminology are often regarded by journalists 'skeptically or [are] altogether ignored'. (Auslander and Gold, 1999: 1396)

At a deeper level, Auslander and Gold note that

numerous opinions have been expressed regarding the need to adopt appropriate terminology when referring to people with disabilities. Yet, there are no clear and consistent findings demonstrating the relationship between inappropriate language and attitudes towards people with disabilities. (Auslander and Gold, 1999: 1397)

Despite these problems, Auslander and Gold, based on their own study, felt that such efforts to improve disability terminology could be undertaken with a better evidence base (including the role of informal as well as formal guideline):

Given the evidence that correct language usage can be successfully taught...the mass media, with its broad exposure and potential influence would seem to be an appropriate place in which to invest such efforts. (Auslander and Gold, 1999: 1404)

More recently, in 2008 Australian academic Shawn Burns undertook a detailed analysis of media guidelines promulgated by the Disability Council of New South Wales (originally in 1994), finding that

> words such as 'Mongoloid' and 'retard' were not used by journalists in a disability context. However, phrases that the guidelines considered to be offensive in the '90s – such as 'wheelchair-bound' and 'suffers from' – are still being used by journalists today. (Burns, 2010: 280)

As there remains a long way to go in the area of news and disability, guidelines certainly have their place, as Burns persuasively argues:

> This is where guidelines...are useful. The guidelines encourage journalists, journalism educators and students to critically appraise the words they use because words are the tools of their trade...Guidelines, like those produced by the Disability Council of NSW, are a means to raise awareness. It would be wrong to consider such guidelines dictatorial (they are called 'guidelines' for a reason) and it would be equally incorrect to dismiss them as acts of 'political correctness'. (Burns, 2010: 281)

While in this area also the picture is unclear, it can be suggested that formal and informal guidelines on representation of people with disabilities in news and media generally have its place. However, today it is clear that such guidelines are only a minor tool in an overall approach – and indeed many of the burning issues for disability and language lie elsewhere, such as language rights for sign language users (Corker, 2000). Indeed, the relationships among language, social practices and identities, politics, and institutions are complex (Wilson and Lewiecki-Wilson, 2001). Add to which, in many important ways, the action on news and disability has moved on – not just because of the changes in news associated with digital platforms and business models but also because of the tectonic political, social, and cultural shifts to which news media have been forced to respond. The prestigious mainstream news media long thought to define the nature of journalism have neither generated these changes, nor have they been their key outlet. Rather, the momentum has come from other areas of news and media – such as sport and entertainment. An excellent case study of these dynamics can be found in one of the biggest global media events involving disability, the Paralympics.

'A Brave New World'?: Disability News in the 2012 London Paralympics

Sport is an important part of society, and it is very big business for media (Miller et al., 2001; Boyle and Haynes, 2009). Despite oft-expressed concerns, consistently high proportions of people around the world participate in sport, including people with disabilities. Many more people (disabled and non-disabled people alike) watch sport – elite sport being excellent fodder as an intensely consumed spectator sport. Sport is a staple across most media forms and especially dominates broadcasting, print, online, and now mobile media (Hutchins and Rowe, 2012; Rowe, 2012; Hutchins and Rowe, 2013). Key battles over new media often revolve around deals to cover sport – witness the spats over broadcast rights for sport in digital media platforms. Despite the capacity of the Internet to support circulation of content by anyone who chooses to do so now, sports organizations strive to control broadcast – only permitting authorized journalists, media, and rights holders to record and distribute images and content (Lefever, 2012).

A prime quality of sport that makes it strategically desirable in the convergent digital environment is not only the fact that sport draws huge numbers of fans, who love the ritual of watching games; it also has to do with the fact that sport involves events – and especially big events. In the media world, where lucrative content can be subject to unauthorized download by users and viewers expect to be able to catch up or view programmes wherever they wish, and generally the idea of paid-for, scheduled media is under intense pressure from consumers, then events are seen by many in the industry as the holy grail. If people are desperate to listen to, watch, or read about events, then they are probably likely to pay something to do so, even in the widespread expectation, supported by the Internet, that media should be free. Sport provides many media events – some of them truly massive, on a global scale. The biggest media events are sporting events: World Cup soccer; US Super Bowl football; basketball; Formula 1 Grand Prix car racing; Wimbledon tennis; sumo wrestling; and new e-sports, such as the Korean Starcraft and Warcraft III phenomenon. At the pinnacle of sports and media are the Olympics.

In scale, scope, and popularity, the Olympics remain unparalleled as a media event. Media events came to the notice of media scholars especially through the classic work of Dayan and Katz, which explored the striking nature of particular events as societal rituals, which in the late 20th century were bound up with, and communicated by, the media.

Since the changes associated with globalization – especially the transformations in media and its societal roles since the early 1990s (Wark, 1994), when Dayan and Katz published their classic study (Dayan and Katz, 1992), scholars have sought to account for the much more dispersed global media systems on the one hand, and the persistence of media events on the other (Couldry, Hepp, and Krotz, 2010). With its roots in ancient Greek sport, the Olympics has become a genuinely international movement – and one in which national identities, tensions, and clashes strongly play out (Price and Dayan, 2008). To host the Olympics is a mammoth undertaking for a country, or host city, and a crucial element of such hospitality involves constructing a veritable media city. The broadcast and other media-related rights to the Olympics are lucrative and tightly guarded. The Olympics is big business and looms large in terms of media economics specifically (Gratton et al., 2012). Mixed with the economics of the Olympics is its role as a source of great national pride, one of the great occasions for countries to communicate meanings about themselves via global media.

Thus, the contemporary Olympics is a blaze of symbols, signs, and representations about what matters to societies and their members (Tomlinson and Young, 2005) – and, beyond this, what it is to be human. The Olympics is taken to be the ultimate test of human strength, endurance, and limitations. They balance individual striving and teamwork, collaboration and competition. Furious debates ensue about the role of science and technology in assisting performance, versus 'cheating' – whether in the form of drugs, bodysuits for swimmers, or equipment that goes beyond the allowed limits. The opening and closing ceremonies of the Olympics are theatrical in every sense of the word: lavish, highly choreographed ceremonies that present the host nation's stories, successes, and challenges and also meditate on the role of sport in human life and society (Tzanelli, 2013). Thus, the 2012 London Olympics paid 'tribute to British heritage and culture, from agrarian beginnings through pop culture successes like The Beatles and J.K. Rowling' (Taylor, 2012). The Olympics also turns out to be a very important place to understand where disability fits into society and media.

To start with, the Olympics still excludes many athletes with disability. For athletes whose impairments impinge on, or preclude them, from competing in sports at the Olympics, they are required to participate in a separate event – the Paralympics (or another event, the Special Olympics) (Thomas and Smith, 2009). The Paralympics has its own rules, aimed to ensure an equal playing field, as it were, among classes of athletes with particular impairments. For many years, the

Paralympics was near invisible, in both society and the media, as a serious sporting or spectatorial event. In recent years, the country hosting the Olympics also hosted the Paralympics, which followed closely on the heels of the main event. However, the way the Paralympics was portrayed was, in a word, 'disabling'. As noted, the events for athletes with disability are segregated from the Olympics, to be held in the separate event of the Paralympics, whereas it is perfectly possible for them to be held as part of one integrated events, just as separate events for men and women form part of the Olympics. Very few people were interested in the Paralympics, and it received little financial support, promotion, and media. Add to which, the news coverage of Paralympics was dominated by the frames, images, and metaphors that we have outlined earlier in this chapter (and book), singing the praise of the brave athletes overcoming their disability. In 2000, one of us, with the late disability scholar, Christopher Newell, undertook a study of the media coverage of the Sydney Olympics and Paralympics, suggesting that

> [t]here is a case to be made that media reporting on the Paralympics, when it does occur, increasingly problematises received notions of disability, producing complex, contradictory media texts ... many stories still draw on stock stereotypes of 'brave, elite athletes', 'special people', 'remarkable achievers' ... (Goggin and Newell, 2000: 78)

The vision from Sydney in 2000 seemed bleak:

> Reporting on the Paralympics has tended to safely remain a restricted, special case of marginalist sport which need not upset the enduring general economy of ableist media representations of disability. (Goggin and Newell, 2000: 80)

The argument Goggin made with Newell was that the governing myth of the paralympic media coverage was quite a cosy one for society at large, namely, that the

> very notion of elite athletes who overcome their disability fits well within the established power relations and norms which actually oppress people with disability in society. These norms take disability to inhere in the individual – rather than to be created by society. (Goggin and Newell, 2000: 80)

Debate raged in ensuing years, around the 2004 and 2008 Olympics and Paralympics (see, for example, Gilbert and Schantz, 2008; Peers,

2009; Legg and Steadward, 2011). By the middle of the second decade of the 21st century, surely things have radically changed, right? Well, not exactly, as we shall discover.

Certainly, things have improved markedly in terms of the Paralympics' place in sport and media. In the 2012 London games, the Paralympics became much more a co-joined part of the Olympics proper. The 2012 Paralympics received unprecedented media attention – often reported as a substantial sporting event in its own right (on this development, see Howe, 2008). While its audiences still fell well below the measures of counterpart Olympic events, the audiences for some Paralympic events were substantial. Genuine attempts were made by journalists to understand, report, and cover such sport and athletes participating in the Paralympics beyond stereotypes and offensive, patronizing language. Media outlets and organizations extended many of the genres of sports coverage to the Paralympics, notably the 'soft' news current affairs, chat, satire and comedy, entertainment 'new' news formats and genre, as well as the well-established 'hard' news. For all this, fundamental contradictions remained.

The promises – as well as the shortcomings – of the Paralympics and its media coverage are evident in the wonderful Opening Ceremony. Something of a tour de force, nonetheless as new 'enlightenment' (the theme for the ceremony), the 2012 Paralympics Opening Ceremony also raised as many questions about disability as society as it represented a new dawn in olympism. The coming home of the Paralympics (which started in Stoke Mandeville in England in 1948) began with celebrated physicist Stephen Hawking urging athletes to 'look at the stars, not your feet'. From there on, the theme of science's role in the limitless potential of human discovery and inventiveness was threaded into a dazzling spectacle. Sir Isaac Newton and the discovery of gravitation were brought to life through the humble apple, a revolving book showing the text of the Universal Declaration of Human Rights. Courtesy of William Shakespeare's *The Tempest*, the ceremony had a play within a play – a clever twist with Prospero (played by Sir Ian McKellen) and a disabled Miranda (Nicola Miles-Wilden), declaring: 'Oh brave new world, that has such people in't'. Prospero's books took on a huge form, followed by a succession of great moments in science, culminating with the Big Bang. The parade of the athletes themselves, always an extended affair, came to a rousing climax with the entrance of the Great Britain team, resplendent in gold and white outfits, grooving to David Bowie's immortal line: 'we can be heroes, just for one day'. The great flourishing of creativity, long incubated in the disability arts movement, took centre stage with a beautiful solo dance by David Toole, Ian Drury's 'Spasticus

Austisticus' performed by Graear Theatre Company, and the flawless voice of blind opera singer Denise Leigh was simultaneously interpreted into sign language.

Much of the power of the event had to do with the recognition of our social diversity. Finally, we can now see a greater breadth of people with disabilities centre stage, with starring roles, in such official rituals and global media events. In this respect, the singing of the national anthem in sign language, as well as with raised voice – to the Queen, the royal party, assembled dignitaries, and a packed stadium – held an importance all of its own. Yet this magic celebration also powerfully presented the central tensions and problems with the state of play in disability and society.

Compared to the Sydney Paralympics in 2000, athletes with disability are covered in ways more consistent with coverage of other elite spokespeople (Howe, 2008). We don't hear so much about the 'brave' athletes 'overcoming' their disability. Just as other athletes enjoy celebrity, many athletes with disability have assumed celebrity also. Media have often found it difficult to cast people with disabilities as celebrity, with rare instances – such as famous actor Christophe Reeve – typically framed in terms of narrow norms. The growing interest and mediation of the Paralympics has broken new ground, whereby the bodies, identities, stories, and quirks of a group of people with disabilities have become famous and offered a bridge for the making of celebrities. The Paralympics has tentatively demonstrated that there are media audiences for disability performances and stories, and, at the intersection of brands, products, biographies, and fames, celebrity for some has followed. Celebrities are our contemporary version of heroes and villains, and sporting heroes count among the most compelling stars of all.

For all the advances in disability and media that the Paralympics embodies, the social imagination of disability, and the way much media still reflects this, takes strange forms indeed. 'Brave' athletes have been edged out by 'superhumans' (as the British Paralympics video would have it), with the 'supercrip' frame and discourse still influential (Silva and Howe, 2012; Misener, 2013). Many media commentators still often found themselves without the ideas, frameworks, or cultural scripts to communicate not only the important events unfolding, as evident in the Opening and Closing Ceremonies especially, but also the coverage generally. We might reflect that the transcendence of the soaring dancers and athletes in today's ceremony – courtesy of the Aerobility charity flying towards the celestial realm – represents an old, double-edged myth of disability. It is certainly an evocative way to imagine the plumbing of the mysteries of the universe, as well as exploring our limits as humans. It might also be about the desire to lift us away from what it is to be mortal and all too human, and the lived realities of disability. The brave new world of disability lies precisely in this double bind. Disability, as the Paralympics can show us, is becoming the new normal.

Too often still the recognition and acceptance of disability still stays within the boundaries of celebration of 'overcoming', of 'transcending', that is, of leaving behind, forgetting, and erasing what troubles us. Here the contemporary media portrayal of Paralympics has ushered elite disability sport and some of favoured representatives into the ranks of elite sportsmen and, to a lesser extent, sportswomen. Like the vexed topics of gender or race in sport, we confront an uneasy alliance between non-disabled and disabled, between what's normal still – a perfect body, without major defects, impairments, illness, deformities, or weakness – and what's becoming more normal, though still troublingly disabled, the bodies of elite athletes with disability.

Disability at the cherished heart of sporting prowess still holds great power to challenge our cherished ideals of who we are – and should be – not only as individuals but also as imagined national and international community. It is not surprising that our ways of talking about disability, as evidenced by sports news and media, still lag well behind the social transformations and radical dynamics that are well underway and irreversible – and stand to enlarge, for the better, our notions of what it is to be human.

Conclusion

News is an area of enormous change in contemporary media. The preferred ways we consume our news have changed significantly. Many of us prefer our news to be entertaining and available when we want it. Yet alongside this, many like to mix satirical, comedy, parody, and tabloid news formats with traditional 'high brow' press and broadcasting news and current affairs. There are new, enhanced roles for intimate, everyday news, as well as ordinary people to report, circulate, and shape news. These transformations mean that the ways that established and emerging news media represent disability are also changing.

As we have outlined, there are distinctive, well-established ways that disability is framed for the purposes of news. While there is great recognition of the problematic aspects of these ways of seeing disability as news, journalism and media production is changing only slowly. So we have provided some examples of contemporary cases of disability in the news to show not only the advances but also the new, crippling norms that are evident. We have focused on sport, because it is often not regarded as 'serious' news. Due to its social prominence, and its dependence on media, sport provides a fertile laboratory for analysing disability representations. We will continue this discussion of representations of disability in Chapter 5, with a focus on another central area of media – television.

5 Beyond Disabled Broadcasting

Television is an important site of media consumption. Earlier in this book we remarked on the contemporary ubiquity of the media – that is, the ways in which much of what we 'learn' about disability, we do so from the media. We have also argued that the consequences of this are much more far-reaching than is commonly realized – ideas that we gain through this everyday media 'teach' us about what is 'human', 'normal', and acceptable, and our attitude to disability is no exception. Sociologist Tim Dant argues that, especially with the decline and displacement of nation states, television is highly influential in shaping our moral and ethical values – what he calls our 'moral imaginary' (Dant, 2012). Television's role in such imagination of morals, we'd suggest, very much extends to disability. Yet like other areas of media, there is little critical analysis of the important role that disability plays – not just in television content, programmes, or practices but arguably also in structuring the medium itself.

An obvious issue with contemporary television is the underrepresentation of actors with disability and also stories that engage disability. This point is made by the annual report of equity and diversity in the media by the Gay and Lesbian Alliance against Defamation (GLAAD) organization:

> In terms of who is showing up and what stories are being shown on our scripted television shows, I think the numbers speak for themselves: it is an embarrassing and completely inaccurate representation of the world around us. Certainly, there are a few bright spots on network television and, in particular, in cable series, but overall, there is a lot of work to do.... To achieve real and lasting change, we must focus not only on hiring performers with disability for roles written with a specific disability but also on ensuring that these performers have a fair shot to play any character, regardless of disability. (Adam Moore, National EEO and Diversity Director for US organization SAG-AFTRA, quoted in GLAAD, 2012: 15)

One of the 'bright spots' that Moore refers to – giving a 'fair shot' for actors with disabilities – is the acclaimed US TV series *Breaking Bad* (2008–2013). *Breaking Bad* is notable as one of the few television series to hire an actor with disability to portray a character with disability: actor R. J. Mitte, who portrayed Walt Junior, has cerebral palsy himself. In addition to this significant example of disability employment in popular television, *Breaking Bad* offers important representations of disability and the disability experience. In the especially memorable first episode of the first season of the series, Walt Senior confronts teenagers for bullying his son in a clothing store. Here we find a vivid recognition of the difficulties and discrimination people with disability experience in everyday public life. As Walt pushes the ringleader to the floor stepping on his head, the teenager describes him as 'psycho' – an ambiguous foreshadowing of Walt's future metamorphosis to notorious drug lord Heisenberg. As the series progresses, however, Walt Junior's disability becomes secondary to his character. As well as its spectacular and gut-wrenching violence, *Breaking Bad* is better known for its exploration of the consequences of a life lived with regrets, as well as its encouragement of its viewers to question where we draw the line on social un/acceptability (Koepsell and Arp, 2012; Logan, 2013). The lesser known story is that *Breaking Bad* also shows that disability can be an integral part of a character, and the social diversity portrayed by a highly significant television show.

Breaking Bad amassed an enormous cult following (Abbott, 2010; Lavery, 2010) and is one of the well-funded, cleverly scripted, imaginatively conceived series, with strong values, exemplary of the emergence of this kind of television taking the place in culture formerly ascribed to cinema (Weissmann, 2012). The rise of these long-form television series – binge-watched courtesy of DVD box sets, downloaded whole series, or through 'season passes' on subscription or online TV (such as iTunes) – has been hailed as auguring something like a 'novelization' of television, with commentators talking about the 'DVD novel' (Metcalf, 2012). The combination of changes in technology, distribution, production, economics, and taste – not least the socio-cultural changes associated with digital formats such as DVD (Bennett and Brown, 2008) and MPEG, Internet, and mobile television – have resulted in a widening of the forms and texts of television series (Curtin, Holt, and Sanson, 2014, Holt and Sanson, 2014). Comics, novels, fan sites, and other forms of new media, not just 'ancillary', are an integral part of making television and its meanings, and how audiences consume and do things with it – what M.J. Clarke calls 'transmedia television' (Clarke, 2012).

Arguably, these developments in television provide enhanced capacity to draw viewers in and make them care about what happens to characters over a long period of time, holding great potential for depictions of disability. Characters can be shown as developing and growing, coming to terms with how to live with an acquired disability like Jason Street on *Friday Night Lights* or like Walt Junior on *Breaking Bad*; the disability is just part of who they are and is not necessarily emphasized. This disability legacy continues in other well-funded, cleverly scripted, imaginatively conceived series such as *Game of Thrones* and *Orange Is the New Black*.

This discussion of how disability figures in a widely watched and discussed American television series provides a lead-in to the topic of this chapter. As we have seen so far in this book, there is a long history of very interesting experiments regarding disability in the highly influential arena of broadcast media. This chapter will offer a snapshot of the state of play when it comes to broadcasting and disability, focusing on television as a popular medium. Our assessment is that disability on television – like disability in broader media and society – is at a crossroads. At the same time that disability is still used to shape narrow ideas about normalcy, it increasingly signals towards prospects for change.

What Do We Know about Disability and TV?

While we largely approach the topic of disability and the media from a North American, British, and Australian perspective, studies from other countries have found similar tendencies, especially in terms of the representation of disability on television. For example, Amit Kama's analysis of Israeli audiences with disabilities found that two stereotypes – inspiration and tragedy – dominated (Kama, 2004). The German study *Disability in Television* likewise found significant connections between the social position of people with disability and the way they were represented on television (Bosee, 2006). Similarly, a study of the representation of disability on prime-time Japanese television between 1993 and 2002 found that disability was under-represented (Saito and Ishiyama, 2005). The authors argued that it would potentially take just one or two main characters with a disability on television to change social attitudes and increase employment opportunities. They recommend adding disability voices to every stage of the media production cycle to change the way disability figures on television (Saito and Ishiyama, 2005). A recent Kenyan study also found that media representation reinforced stigma against people with disability (Inimah, Mukulu, and Mathooko, 2012).

These studies from different countries are the most recently available, but Guy Cumberbatch and Ralph Negrine's 1988 content analysis of disability on British prime-time television over a six-week period remains the most comprehensive investigation of disability on television to date (Cumberbatch and Negrine, 1992). This was a full quantitative and qualitative study of disability on television, highlighting what the authors describe as stereotypes and inconsistencies. They found stark contrasts between the portrayal of people with disability and those without. Their analysis showed that people with disability were often portrayed in derisory ways on broadcast television. Reflecting on their findings, Cumberbatch and Negrine made several recommendations regarding the way forward for disability representation on broadcast television such as giving people with disability the opportunity to become among the leading characters on television. Were this to occur, they argued, disability would come to be seen as an ordinary experience by the general public.

In placing this kind of approach historically, it is worth noting that Cumberbatch and Negrine's research was conducted during the mid to late 1980s when a 'people first' ethos was a key 'liberal exhortation' influential in disability rights. On this view, people with disability should be seen as people first and their disability regarded as incidental: 'Given that people with disabilities wish to be treated first and foremost as people, and only secondarily as people who happen to have disabilities, they should be so treated on television' (Cumberbatch and Negrine, 1992: 141). In the intervening two or so decades, the complexity of representing people as *just* people has become much more apparent, not least through the great experiment of 'reality television' (Turner, 2009).

Reality television has been a dynamic, popular area of television since the late 1990s. Reality television is now an international and transnational phenomenon, involved in a lucrative trade in formats that have seen fascinating twists on reality TV across Africa, the Middle East, Oceania, as well as the regions in which it originated such as South America, North America, and Europe. Reality has been widely debated and discussed, not least for its achievement – or at least potential– to broaden the bandwidth for overdue representations of the messy diversity and realities of ordinary people and their everyday lives (Creed, 2003; Turner, 2009; Müller, Klijn, and Van Zoonen, 2012). Reality television has often broken new ground with the representation of gays and lesbians, working class, immigrants and refugees, people with a range of political views, people outside the narrow range of ethnic and racial types that dominate much of television (GLAAD, 2012). Often tightly scripted, cast, and produced, reality television has also been identified as offering the potential for a different representation of disability that recognizes both the effects of impairment as well as social disablement (Ellis, 2015; Rodan, Ellis and Lebeck, 2014).

Although young, attractive, white, non-disabled people feature most often on reality television in Western countries (despite its aspirations, as noted, to expand the diversity), there has been the occasional contestant with a disability on shows such as *Survivor, The Amazing Race, America's Next Top Model, American Idol, Masterchef, The Biggest Loser, Project Runway,* and *Big Brother.* In a study of the representation of disability in reality TV, Floris Müller, Marlies Klijn, and Lisbet van Zoonen found that reality television has the potential to educate people with little experience with disability through both incidentalist and non-incidentalist strategies of representation. The obvious point, we would make also, is the paradox of disability as often being important, if not fundamental, to a person's identity, or how they are positioned in society, or placed in relation to its power structures (what has been termed theoretically as 'subjectivity'). So while disability is sometimes incidental, this is not always the case and a corrective overemphasis on disability as incidental could impact the social problem of disability (Müller, Klijn, and Van Zoonen, 2012). In other words, sometimes people with disabilities need to have their impairments acknowledged and compensated through alternative formats such as Braille to have a commensurate experience as people without any impairment. If people with disability are always represented as 'just people' then these entitlements could become harder to come by.

While an updated, suitably recast comprehensive study of disability on television has not been conducted (at least for English-language television), there is a US-advocacy group study that gives much food for thought. In 2010, the US-based GLAAD began analysing the disability diversity of regular characters found in various types and genres of US television series alongside their analysis of the sexual, racial, and ethnic diversity. In the analysis of 2010–2011 television schedules, they found only 1% of series regular characters had a disability. Of the 587 characters they researched, only six, including Dr House and Dr Remy 'Thirteen' Hadley from *House, Glee's* Artie Abrams, Saul from *Brothers and Sisters,* Max Braverman from *Parenthood,* and Dr. Albert Robbins from *CSI: Crime Scene Investigation,* had a disability (GLAAD, 2010). Two years later, in the 2012–2013 season, the number of regular characters depicted with disabilities had dropped to only four – or 0.6% of all characters (GLAAD, 2012). Two of these were gay and lesbian characters with disability – *Nurse Jackie*'s Thor Lundgren and Arizona from *Grey's Anatomy*. This contrasts to some 12% of US citizens living with a disability. GLAAD observe that reality television programming, although holding great potential for diversity of representation, does not release participant information early enough to be included in the study. In its count, however, GLAAD had boosted the odds by also including people living with 'non-apparent disabilities' such as cancer or HIV/AIDS – that is, types of disabilities covered under the Americans with Disabilities Act (ADA) (GLAAD, 2012). To no avail, as the striking disparity between the relative substantial proportion of Americans with disabilities – the 'American Scene', as one advocacy leader quoted in the GLAAD study puts it (GLAAD, 2012: 15) – and their miniscule representation as regular television characters, appears to hold fast.

Disabling Images and Disabled Audiences

With the influential work of theorists such as Ien Ang (Ang, 1991), David Morley (2009), and Charlotte Brunsdon (1978), much research shifted to audience constitution, consumption, and material practices as critical to understanding to what television actually amounted. Thus far, however, there has been surprisingly little empirical or theoretical research on disabled audiences, or what sense audiences make of disability. Karen Ross' pioneering 1997 paper still stands as a rare investigation of disability audiences (Ross, 1997). Intended as a counter to the emphasis on content analysis in disability theorization outlined above, Ross proceeded from the standpoint that disability is absent on television and held focus groups to discover what audiences with disabilities thought. Interestingly, however, the participants with disability in her study focused on stereotypes of people with disability as criminals or outcasts, especially within soap operas. The participants saw these images as contributing to their social marginalization (Ross, 1997).

While it is a commonplace argument that audiences are active in the meanings they make from television, interpreting images according to their context and experiences (Livingstone, 1998), the constant repetition of certain imagery reinforces television's *symbolic power* to 'speak for us all' (Gray, 2008). Gray argues that through sheer repetition these images have communicative power to create a dominant image of disability. In a more recent study of audience reception of soap opera, Alison Wilde discovered that the repetition of imagery within the soap opera genre that positioned disability as outside the boundaries of normality also impacted on audience members with disability who most often identified with non-disabled characters (Wilde, 2004). These audiences also recognized that disability was used as a vehicle within narratives to explore other issues (Wilde, 2004). US critical theorists David Mitchell and Sharon Snyder call this use of disability a 'narrative prosthesis', making a pun on the role that a prosthesis – a crutch, artificial limb, or other kind of prop – plays when it comes to disability. For Mitchell and Snyder, a 'narrative prosthesis' functions as

> a character-making trope in the writer's arsenal, as a social category of deviance, as a symbolic vehicle for meaning-making and cultural critique, and as an option in the narrative negotiation of disabled subjectivity. (Mitchell and Snyder, 2000: 1)

What Mitchell and Snyder are pointing out is the customary way that storylines and other aspects of narrative hinge on disability. For example, many a narrative, particularly in the medical drama, is generated from characters suffering an incident, so creating the interruption from their previous lives – and give rise to a drama. Attention to the function of disability to structure and support the story in television narratives allows us to make sense of the gradual increase of major and minor characters with disability on television, who, through their sheer volume, as well as by the crucial role they play, add weight and variation to representational strategies of disability.

A comprehensive analysis of such representation is sorely needed in order to address the difficult methodological issues of how to properly account for the way that people with disabilities feature across all aspects of broadcast television, including as both regular and 'non-regular' characters. Also, and perhaps more pressing, it is needed in order to analyse the way that disability functions on contemporary television, much of which is now consumed via new genres, formats, and technologies, such as Internet and mobile platforms – the new television *ecologies*, rather than the stand-alone television box and broadcast network of the past (Abruzzese et al., 2012).

While the research is simply not available, our sense is that while the numbers of regular characters highlighted by studies such as the GLAAD count are unacceptably low, disability is becoming both more visible and more culturally 'legible' in television. That is, there's more disability in television and audiences are both more interested and expert in 'reading' it. This is how we would interpret the findings of a 2012 study, which notes that characters with disability, although still proportionally less than the incidence of people with disability in the community, are now shown on television with more complex lives than ever before (Luther, Lepre, and Clark, 2011). Indeed, disability is visible in shows across a number of formats and genres including historical drama (*Downtown Abby, Call the Midwives*), medical drama (*House, Chicago Hope, Grey's Anatomy*), satire (*Weeds, Scrubs*), musical (*Glee*), reality TV (*Push Girls, Britain's Missing Top Model, Little People Big World*) and programming designed for newer television platforms (*Game of Thrones, Orange Is the New Black*).

Representation

Representations are always complex expressions and articulations, images, stories, and narratives. Representations are also key ways in which we imagine ourselves with others. The understanding we gain from the media is further reflected within society, including in the experiences we encounter with disability, and the policies, laws, and practices that govern the lives of people with disabilities. For example, an early 1990s study of nurses found that, despite professional experience to the contrary, the frequently espoused media stereotype that people with mental health conditions were a violent threat was believed by these health professionals (Philo et al., 1994). A 2012 collection on mental illness in popular media offers a range of perspectives on how such 'disorders' are represented (Rubin, 2012). Thus, there are good reasons to take seriously the notion that representation is intimately involved in policing the boundaries of how we relate to disability, and indeed what is accepted as 'normal' in our societies.

A good example of the complexities of representation is to be found in the US series *Glee*. *Glee* seeks to represent and engage with the multicultural, diverse society in which it is set through a focus on diversity and high school outcasts finding purpose and belonging with their high school show choir (Glee Club) and its advisor Will Schuster. *Glee* is often criticized for being tokenistic in its stereotypical portrayal of minority groups, not least when it comes to disability. Take the case of disabled character Artie, whose interactions in the Glee group are minor – mostly one-liners – until episode 9 'Wheels' in the first season. The 'Wheels' episode explicitly addresses the new societal expectations – 'political correctness', if you will – concerning disability.

As Will exhorts the club to embrace 'accessible songs' familiar to judges of an impending competition, Artie's experiences with disability become a narrative prosthesis to stimulate an exploration of a number of 'accessibility' issues in 'Wheels'. However, Artie's experiences are rendered a poor second as the non-disabled members of the group dominate the episode. A case in point is when Will forces them to spend three hours a day in wheelchairs. The other students are initially apathetic to the fact that Artie is unable to join them on the inaccessible bus ride to the competition, and so he is effectively excluded. They continue to ignore him, as he attempts to teach them wheelchair dancing moves. Ultimately, though, they decide to perform the competition piece *Proud Mary* in wheelchairs after all. Despite this, there is a strong sense in which this performance reaffirms the importance of the non-disabled performers' abilities, rather than those of Artie. For instance, although Artie is the male lead in this performance, there are no close ups of him singing. Instead, Artie is just one of a rather large group of singers in wheelchairs who wheel around the stage high fiving each other.

In the following episodes, Artie recedes into the background until the episode 'Dream On' which features another highly controversial depiction of disability (episode 19, series 1) when Artie imagines that he has been cured and is able to achieve his dream of being a dancer who does not have to use his wheelchair. The dream is motivated by an awkward attempt at romance with fellow Glee Club member Tina. When the pair are unable to dance together due to Artie's impairments, Tina begins to research cures for spinal cord injury. She discovers research into electrical currents and stem cells and informs Artie medical trials are showing promising results. Artie and Tina then appear in the next scene at a large shopping mall, where Artie has just purchased tap shoes. Artie tells Tina he has started on the therapies she discovered and they're working. He gets up out of his chair and leads a flash mob in the widely viewed 'Safety Dance' number. At the end of the performance, however, Artie lands back in his chair in a thud: it was a dream after all.

To find a way forward, Artie discusses Tina's research with Emma, the school's quirky guidance counsellor (who incidentally has obsessive compulsive disorder (OCD)). She cautions him against false hope and reminds Artie that the damage to his spinal cord is severe and irreversible and that the studies are not even in their infancy. Instead of pinning his hopes on a potentially long way off cure, Emma suggests Artie see her once a week for a while. Artie gives up on his dream and tells Tina he can't dance with her because he needs to focus on dreams that can come true.

The contrast between these two episodes of *Glee* is quite telling, yet both are different facets of the typically narrow way in which disability is imagined across much of the media. Thus, in *Glee*, we would suggest that the possible worlds of disability – and indeed society generally – are impoverished and narrow. The 'social imaginary' of disability thus puts real limits on the life chances and possibilities of all participants. Consider, for instance, that Emma counsels Artie to aspire to wheelchair dancing (now an elite sport) as a way for him to achieve his dream rather than give up on them as hopeless.

Disability on television allows us to reflect on the ways a particular era or culture value their disabled members. The medium exposes both key moments in disability social justice, and the resistance to social change. The cult television series *Star Trek* offers a clear illustration of this. For example, in the 1966 episode 'The Menagerie', Captain Christopher Pike, who is injured following exposure to delta rays, operates as a clear source of discomfort within the narrative, particularly to his protégé Captain Kirk. As a result of his injuries, Pike is badly burnt and unable to walk or talk. His only means of communication is via brain waves that allow him to operate a light at the front of his wheelchair (which incidentally totally encases his body). At the conclusion of the episode, Pike elects to live in captivity on a planet where he will be granted an illusion of youth and ability. Moving into *Star Trek Next Generation*, characters such as Geordi La Forge exist with impairments and make use of technology to mitigate their effects. He wears a thin curved glasses-like device (so-called visual instrument and sensory organ replacement (VISOR) across his eyes, which provide him with an artificial sense of sight). Geordi's VISOR also affords him a sense of sight beyond normal human capabilities, for example he is able to 'see' vital signs such as heart rate and temperature, thus allowing him to detect mood and when humans are being deceitful. Geordi refused to be cured twice in the series. The changes in the ways disability is imagined within the worlds of *Star Trek* reveal a shifting social, cultural, and technological landscape.

Further, *The Fugitive* established the effectiveness of disability as shorthand for evil on popular television during the 1960s – a strategy repeated in the 1970s (*Hawaii Five-O*), 1980s (*The Jewell in the Crown*), 1990s (*Law & Order*), and continuing today (*Criminal Minds, Bones*). However, recently a new subcategory of television crime has emerged where the investigators possess impairment, a quality that sometimes improves their ability to solve crime (*Monk, Law & Order Criminal Intent, Criminal Minds, CSI, Silence,* and *Bones*).

A hugely popular genre in television since the medium's inception is the crime drama. Television crime drama often turns on the dialectic between social order being subverted (Forsham, 2012), but then restored even if only as a gesture (Marc, 1984; Potter and Marshall, 2009). So there have been long-standing links between the crime genre, ideology, and society (Sparks, 1992). However, we now have a very wide range of variations to the crime genre, which is a fertile and creative television and cultural form (Effron, 2011). What is less commonly acknowledged and studied is the role of disability in how crime helps us, through the media, to imagine good and evil, right and wrong, ourselves, and our society. Disability is a key feature in the formula and cultural scripts we love in crime drama, and it encompasses all facets of crime drama.

During the 1980s, a number of budget cuts in the United States resulted in decreasing services for people with disabilities and mental health conditions. Roughly at the same time, we see the introduction of the ADA and the rise of the social justice critique focusing on 'people first' approaches to disability. The resulting contradictions can be seen playing out in an early 1990s episode of the popular television show *MacGyver*. In the episode 'There But For the Grace', MacGyver infiltrates a group of homeless people and with the help of Donny (who has a mental health condition) exposes a wealthy businessman for fraudulently claiming homeless and mentally ill as his employees in order to claim government benefits. This kind of episode where a disability issue is explored within a single narrative is something of a set piece or minor genre in its own right – often described as 'very special episodes' and criticized for not considering disability in a serious or sustained way.

In the 2000s, people with disability were portrayed in television series in various guises: low-income employment (*Becker*); leading a highly skilled team of investigators (*CSI*); and working for the President (*The West Wing*). By the 2010s, people with disability had become much more visible – if not, in a certain way, dominating a shifting television landscape: teenagers with acquired disability (*Friday Night Lights, Glee*); those disabled since birth (*Switched at Birth, Breaking Bad*); people in prison and working there (*Oz, Orange Is the New Black*); people with disabilities on the side of the law (*Monk*) and against it (*Bones, Castle*). This very brief recital of representations of disability on the US television also serves to remind us that, as yet, the history of disability on television is under-recognized and little documented. There may well be troubling reasons why this is so, evoked, for instance, of historian Paul Longmore's famous suggestion that audiences 'screen' the image of disability out of their consciousness for fear of becoming disabled themselves (Longmore, 2003: 132).

One of the characteristics of television is its long history of repetition, ritual, innovation, and renewal by following and then breaking formulas. As we have argued throughout this book, the media often follows particular formulas or cultural scripts about disability that ascribe to medicalized discourses of tragedy and inspiration. This is especially true about television. However, we find ourselves in a moment of significant change in television, which, in turn, has influenced the way disability is popularly imagined. Television theorists such as Amanda Lotz and John Hartley argue that television has entered a post-broadcast era (Lotz, 2007; Hartley, 2010). Debate continues about the exact nature of contemporary television, not least given its extraordinary resilience. One aspect of the new television mediascapes is that whereas the broadcast era focused on attracting a mass audience through programming which appealed to the dominant cultural values of a large number of people in order to attract advertising dollars, today smaller niche audiences are sought after, which when aggregated actually become quite large. Indeed, it could be plausibly argued that disability is essential to the current moment of television, characterized by edgier, 'high-quality' content such as *Breaking Bad* discussed in the introduction to this chapter.

In this sense, it can be contended that disability structures narratives, provides format innovation, and has been utilized as part of what has hubristically been termed a 'new golden age' or 'revolution' (Sepinwall, 2012). If we take HBO's *The Sopranos* as one beginning of such a sea change, then arguably disability was and is vital to television, which now focuses on niche as much as mass audiences. Recall that *The Sopranos* begins with disability, when mob boss Tony Soprano visits a psychologist to deal with an anxiety disorder. Less well noticed is that throughout its six seasons, *The Sopranos* made use of a large number of minor characters with disability: Beansie Gaeta, a pizzeria owner who became paraplegic following a revenge bashing; Tony Soprano's institutionalized Uncle Hercules; and Svetlana, an amputee Russian nurse caring for Tony's ailing mother.

A conceit of contemporary television discourse is that popular programming such as *Game of Thrones*, *Breaking Bad*, and *True Blood* (among many others) is attributed to the trail blazed by *The Sopranos*. While *The Sopranos* is often heralded as the beginning of a newer 'quality' form of post-broadcast television, it was influenced by earlier drama series such as *Oz* (1997–2003), *St Elsewhere* (1982–1988), and *Twin Peaks* (1990–1991). Interestingly, these shows *also* embraced representations of disability.

For instance, the prison drama *Oz* was narrated by Augustus Hill, a wheelchair-using inmate. According to the show's creator, Tom Fontana, the choice of disabled narrator was significant, as he envisioned a Greek chorus of sorts where 'somebody in the community would step out and talk about themes and bigger ideas' (Fontana quoted in Sepinwall, 2012: 23). Fontana believed this narrator needed experience beyond the prison walls, an experience shaped by minority interests. Although originally conceived of as a racial minority, disability was also incorporated to provide greater depth of characterization. As a wheelchair user, Hill initially does not pose a threat to other inmates or guards but throughout the series experiences conflicts and significant storylines. However, disability culture activist and community artist Petra Kuppers believes that Hill's characterization is shaped by a 'pervasive attitude towards disability as a metaphor and shorthand' and further locates these insightful outsider style of characters as a continuation of disabled performers' cultural function as freaks (Kuppers, 2003: 12).

Disability also occupies a key position in the cult series *Lost*. John Locke finds himself on the island having boarded Oceanic Flight 815, because as a wheelchair user he was denied admission to an Australian walkabout. He experiences a mysterious cure and is constructed as a mystical and spiritual character. Television scholar Jason Mittle argues that Locke's experience with disability and its narrative relevance within the long-form television series worked as a prosthesis to reveal the difference between passengers' pre-crash experiences and their lives on the island (Mittle, 2009).

These examples show that while representations of disability are becoming more popular and visible, they may continue other forms of cultural prejudice. Despite this, clear moments of transgression are recognizable within the narratives, such as when Hill engages in conjugal visits with his wife in *Oz* or when Locke responds to employment discrimination in *Lost*. Similarly, *Twin Peaks* includes a number of characters with disability with complex lives and important characterizations. Disability is often used in *Twin Peaks* to create atmosphere. Take, for example, the eccentric character Nadine Hurley, who wears an eye patch following a hunting accident on her honeymoon. She begins the series obsessed with creating noiseless drape runners, and then, following a suicide attempt, believes she is still a teenager. Her memory loss is attributed to adrenaline. To add to the atmosphere, throughout both seasons Nadine possesses superhuman strength. Nadine is but one character among many with impairment. Other impairments evident in the show's characters include a variety of cognitive impairments, both acquired and lifelong, including anxiety, depression, spinal cord injury, OCD, addiction, agoraphobia, and hearing loss, that contribute to the supernatural atmosphere.

If it is the case that representation of disability on television is becoming richer and more complex, this raises a series of fascinating questions about cultural value that go to the heart of regarding disability as a space for cultural, intellectual, aesthetic, and social engagement, appreciation, and debate. That is, we could make a transformative move – to see disability as a cultural resource, rather than simply signifying our society's worst fears, most oppressive anxieties, and unwished for frailties.

Attention to the function of disability to structure and support the story in television narratives allows us to make sense of the gradual increase of minor characters with disability on television who, through their sheer volume as well as by the crucial role they play, add weight and variation to representational strategies of disability. Despite this, a common vision of disability – that it is tragic, inspirational, or an overcoming story – dominates television and our social understandings of what disability is. It is also continually reproduced throughout social life. Tragic and inspiration themed narratives can further isolate people with disabilities because they present difficult to relate to stories: the person with disability is held to a higher standard to everyone else. Pitched against the grain, new disability humour, on the other hand, challenges ableist conceptions by offering disability as another instance of the shared human experience: an experience that can be laughed at.

A New Phase of Disability Humour: 'I Didn't Come Here to Be Your Mascot'

Humour can be used to expose social problems and confront social taboos, but it can also be used to reinforce existing power relations, social categories, sorting, and order (Germeroth and Shultz, 1998). As we discussed in Chapter 1, for much of the history of disability, humour has played a destructive role, with the joke being 'on' the disability community through sick jokes and disabled 'fools'. In recent times, the influence of disabled comics has become a key way to expose the diversity of people with disability. As Beth Haller explains, we are discouraged from laughing at people with disability because disability is often constructed as tragic (Haller, 2010).

However, according to Haller, a new phase of disability humour characterized by equality is emerging. For Haller, this style of humour is empowering and by allowing people with disability to exert control over their image on television offers a clear counter to destructive humour (Haller, 2010). People with disability take control of their image and, through humour, expose and laugh at society's disabling barriers. Disability humour invites an integrated approach to representation because characters with disability are constructed as just like any other character in the series. Haller explains that disability humour allows everyone to 'laugh at our shared experiences, and having a disability is depicted as just another feature about human beings' (Haller, 2010: 171).

The web series *My Gimpy Life* confronts disabling social attitudes through disability humour. *My Gimpy Life* follows Teal Sherer, an aspiring actress with a disability ('the next Reece Witherspoon'), as she navigates the inaccessible world of Hollywood auditions, productions, and nightlife. For example, following a poor audition, Teal feels uncomfortable and insulted when the director describes her as inspiring and invites her to see the closing night of her Company's latest play *For Colored Girls*. The director is invoking the traditional images of disability and moral imaginary, where disability is figured as inspirational. For example, when Teal meets the cast following the play, they similarly find her inspiring. Teal finds this confronting, and eventually snaps:

It's enough! I'm an actress; I didn't come here to be your mascot. Oh you're so so inspiring, such an inspiration. Do you know how insulting that is? It's like me telling her that you're so well spoken or that you could pass for white or that this is just a wonderful little feminist fubu theatre company. (*My Gimpy Life*, episode 3 'Inspirational')

The black director and actors literally stand aghast that Teal would speak to them in such an unacceptably racist way, but the point is made through humour. We laugh at people's attitudes towards Teal as a wheelchair user throughout the series as she is asked by a random stranger in the street whether she can have sex; auditions for a role in a back alley because she can't get up stairs to see the director; asks a rival if they are about to have a 'dance off' when they argue in a nightclub; claims her disability is a result of a 'sex swing' accident; and is assigned a toilet as her dressing room on a job. Thus, a behind the scenes promo for the series plays off people's discomfort around laughing at, or with, disability. In response to a fan question about whether it is okay to use the word 'gimpy', Teal, who would be racially coded as white, simultaneously invokes empowering disability humour and draws parallels with the ways racial groups have subverted their subjugation: 'I dunno. Is it okay for Jay Z to drop the N bomb so much? I mean I love his new song with Kanye but how am I supposed to request that in a club?' (*My Gimpy Life*, 2012).

My Gimpy Life is but one example of this new genre of television comedy that is emerging around disability humour that allows people with disabilities to take control of their image by inviting largely non-disabled audiences to see the humour in disabling situations. Other shows in this genre include *Legit, The Last Leg*, and *Life's Too Short* – each of which contains imagery and jokes that the producers feared audiences would find offensive. Not unexpectedly, there have been complaints about certain aspects of the new disability humour. For example, host Adam Hills' embrace of disability humour in *The Last Leg*, a British Channel 4 show, which originally ran alongside the 2012 London Paralympics, prompted the Twitter hashtag #isitok ('is it OK?'). Accusations of bad taste, offence, and differing views aside – exactly what edgy humour is supposed to elicit – the embrace of disability issues within everyday life as something to laugh at, and thus provoke reflection and social change, has been in large part embraced (Couch, 2013; Ryan, 2012).

Conclusion: Future Television's Embrace of Disability

At the outset of this chapter, we recalled that in the late 1980s pioneering authors Cumberbatch and Negrine encouraged British television producers to create roles and narratives for people with disability that embraced these people as leading characters. Although the radical social change they predicted has not been achieved, in the intervening 25 or so years there has been limited, though significant, change.

Throughout the chapter, we discussed the way innovative forms of television programming such as *The Sopranos, Twin Peaks, Lost*, and *Breaking Bad* rely on a long established use of disability as part of their visual grammar and as a narrative prosthesis. To reiterate Mitchell and Snyder's point, representations in these shows very clearly reveal the way disability is often invoked on television as 'a social category of deviance, as a symbolic vehicle for meaning-making and cultural critique, and as an option in the narrative negotiation of disabled subjectivity' (Mitchell and Snyder, 2000: 1).

Although disability features prominently in narratives on popular television and across a number of dramatic formats, it continues to be individualized as something to be overcome or cured. When television lacks a number of representations of minority groups, the stereotypes take on greater representational weight (Gray, 2008). While this chapter has discussed a number of characters with disability on television, when considered in the context of the dominating number of non-disabled characters they still remain a minority whose images are densely loaded. Indeed, they are likely to influence future representations.

Moves towards a 'disability culture' can be seen in innovative but not widely viewed programming, such as *My Gimpy Life*. Such programmes make use of disability humour to expose ableism and 'build bridges of understanding' (Haller, 2010: 171) between the disabled and not by presenting disability as another experience of humanity. Yet while there is greater openness on the part of audiences, media producers, and media organizations to such programming that embraces disability as both an integral part of everyday life and, at the same time, an opportunity for cultural experimentation, learning, and entertainment (something which television does do brilliantly), sadly, remains in the margins.

So how can this historic opportunity for the media – society at large and culture in general – embrace the richness, complexity, and difficulties of disability? A central challenge lies in the fact that despite the incorporation of disabled characters, actors, presenters, themes, and awareness into mainstream television, people with disabilities have historically, and still remain, significantly under-represented as owners, managers, professionals, and workers at all levels of media industries. Accordingly, in the next chapter we turn to the great prospects and already demonstrated innovation that can be found in the ways that individuals and groups with disabilities have taken up opportunities to use new digital, informal media to create new kinds of public spheres.

6 Disability and Media Work

We finished the previous chapter with a discussion of the web series *My Gimpy Life*, a comedy loosely based on actress and producer Teal's own life and the 'fun' situations she encounters as she attempts to break into Hollywood. When Teal could not get funding to produce the second season, she turned to online crowd-sourced funding through Kickstarter to continue the programme: *My Gimpy Life* (the second season) reached their Kickstarter goal of US$55,000 in under a month (Sherer, 2013).

The case of *My Gimpy Life* provides a fitting segue to the topic of Chapter 6, disability and media work. In this chapter, we interrogate the lack of employment opportunities for people with disabilities in media industries, contrast this parlous situation with the great prospects and already demonstrated innovative ways in which individuals and groups with disabilities have taken up opportunities to become skilled media workers, and use new digital, informal media to create new kinds of public spheres. In doing so, we approach this emerging new media environment with caution, not least given its continuing difficulties with access.

The headline story concerning training and employment of people with disabilities in the media, as we shall see, is that change is still slow to come in mainstream media industries, though there have been notable exceptions. In order to explore this, the chapter moves on to consider the concerns related to the power issues disabled people have as media employees, and how community-based projects can help overcome some factors. This is a vastly under-researched area and we make recommendations for important future work. From here, we shift to new media technology and disability, where issues of accessibility reappear as pivotal. These ideas are discussed using case studies of disability and new media drawn from the blogosphere, social media, and community television.

The overarching argument of the chapter is that although new opportunities exist for participation, distribution, and exchange, and although people with disabilities have been able to influence the mainstream media in some cases, key questions remain. How is disability communicated via these platforms? Does new media introduce additional forms of social participation for people with disabilities? When people with disabilities are themselves under-represented as producers of media, and media professionals often lack the cultural competence or training to understand disability, how is disability represented?

Training and Employment of People with Disabilities in the Media

The issue of work was discussed by a number of contributors to Nelson's 1994 US collection, with a section looking at the 'reality' of the media as a workplace. Since then there has been a history of at least some mainstream media outlets commissioning research into improving the social position of people with disabilities by increasing media attention and the role employees with disabilities could play in this. For example, the 1998 report into training and equal opportunities in ITV, Channel 4, and Channel 5 in the United Kingdom found that although some regional licences maintained active involvement with disability action groups, 'progress was uneven and generally slow in the employment of disabled people' (Wood, 2012). The report noted, however, that some people with disabilities are provided training through community-based projects and channel-specific initiatives such as Channel 4's involvement with the Employer's Forum on Disability. This forum, recently renamed the Business Disability Forum, is a disability network that seeks to educate employers on the benefits of hiring people with disability within their organizations. Similarly, Channel 5 is a member of the Broadcaster's Disability Network (Ofcom, 1998). This network was involved with the creation of the report *Adjusting the Picture* which we discuss in depth later. Yet, despite such initiatives, over 15 years later only 5.6% of the media industry workforce was estimated to comprise people with disabilities (Brooks et al., 2012).

The role of media, and media representations, in shaping disableist notions of work and employment has been a consistent theme in critical disability research. Increased employment is frequently touted as a potentially positive outcome of improved media representations of disability. It is true that the social model of disability, which we draw upon throughout this book, began with a concern for employment possibilities for people with disabilities and drew attention to the role of media in shaping its conditions (Barnes and Mercer, 2005). However, the focus on mass media imagery constraining the possibility for employment and how we imagine work raises the question – what of notions of work and conditions of employment for people with disability in the media industry itself?

Employer Fear

'Fear' recurs as a significant reason for the poor employment levels of people with disabilities across all industries (Peck and Kirkbride, 2001; Raynor and Hayward, 2009). Employers fear a number of factors, including the costs associated with accommodations, loss of productivity as a result of increased supervision, being unable to terminate a employee with a disability, and the fear that an employee with a disability is of lesser quality than one without (Peck and Kirkbride, 2001). This is true also for the media industries, where people with disabilities are under-represented as workers at all levels. The Canadian Association of Broadcasters (CAB) reports that barriers to employment in media industries centre around:

- opportunities in the broadcasting industry for persons with disabilities;
- attitudes of employers, notably broadcasters;
- issues relating to accommodation in the broadcaster workplace;
- concerns relating to education and training, and the general lack of support from the education system in promoting broadcasting as a career path for students with disabilities; and
- issues regarding the importance of communication and outreach between the disability community and broadcasters. (Cavanagh, Krstic and Steele, 2005)

These barriers all relate to fears about people with disabilities as being unable to contribute to the workforce.

Has the Picture on Media Work and Disability Been Adjusted?

Although now over a decade old, the British report *Adjusting the Picture* is a rare manual on employing people with disabilities in media industries. It focuses on broadcast media – namely radio and television – and recommends producers change their attitudes regarding the abilities of people with disabilities as employees and workers in the media, and further espouses an increased representation of disability. Both *Adjusting the Picture* and the European Commission's *Guide for Media and Disabilities* are now significantly dated. However, regrettably there is no reason to suggest that the key findings aren't still true – especially that people with disabilities are significantly under-represented in the media workforce, and that changing this situation is the responsibility of senior management (Fundación ONCE, 2007).

Both reports blame the industry's reliance on freelancers and short-term employment for the inequitable workforce and disabling employment practices (Blake and Stevens, 2004; Fundación ONCE, 2007). *Adjusting the Picture* specifically addresses the issue of fear and the misconception that employing people with disabilities will result in an increased cost and workload for other staff by listing reported fears specific to the media (Blake and Stevens, 2004). The report identifies some simple accommodations that can be made to increase the employment of people with disabilities in the media as both behind-the-scene and on-screen workers (Blake and Stevens, 2004). It also notes that the majority of people with disabilities do not require onerous accommodations. It also explains any costs associated with workplace accommodations can be reimbursed through government grants (Peck and Kirkbride, 2001).

The disabling barriers experienced by people with disabilities attempting to enter media industries – at all levels and in both on-screen and behind-the-scene roles – can be further illustrated by research Gerard Goggin, Christopher Newell, and Sue Salthouse did into the Australian industry in 2002. They interviewed members of the Australian film and television industry regarding employment and training opportunities for people with disabilities. They spoke to industry figures with and without disabilities and found that, while pathways to entry were diverse, many structural barriers prevented people with disabilities from fully participating. These included consideration of attitudes, barriers, and lack of resources, as well as barriers relating to disabling attitudes and limited facilities. In an extremely competitive industry, people with disability are often not encouraged to seek training or employment (Goggin and Newell, 2003b). Whereas Goggin and Newell looked at both behind-the-screen and on-screen roles, Lori Breeden focused exclusively on actors with disabilities seeking work in Los Angeles and found similar tendencies (Breeden, 2012). Regrettably we were not able to find any other research on disability, work, and training in media industries – something that urgently needs to be remedied, along with the other yawning gaps that characterize many areas of disability and work research (Jones and Wass, 2013).

Acting as if Disability Mattered

Increasing on-screen representation of disability is cited as one way to increase the employment of people with disabilities in broader society; however, actors with disabilities claim a prejudice against them in the industry and are reluctant to ask for simple accommodations. Again, available research is scant, and the handful of studies are limited in conceptualization, approach, and methods. One of the few available studies, a 2005 Screen Actors Guild (SAG) investigation into the employment of actors with disabilities, revealed a substantial bias against actors with disability. It reported that actors with disability worked fewer days or not at all, with many reporting workplace discrimination. Prospects for employment were seen as limited due to a perceived lack of acting jobs in general, difficulties in getting an audition, and because actors with a disability believed they were only being considered for disability-specific roles (Armbrust, 2005). Simon McKeown and Paul Darke outline the problems faced by disabled actors in the context of the broader cultural concern of increasing disability representation both behind and on screen:

> When disabled actors do get a chance to play on mainstream screens they are often compromised before the program begins by limited or stereotyped roles, reduced bargaining power, lower pay, even lower investments in their career promotion by industry insiders, and pervasive discrimination in casting regardless of acting talent or experience. (McKeown and Darke, 2013: 156)

In a 2012 study, actors with disabilities report that they are overlooked for both mainstream roles and also disability-specific ones (Breeden, 2012). This is certainly a concern that emerges anecdotally and in available public commentary. For instance, as we discussed in Chapter 5, the popular television show *Glee* was often criticized during its first season for hiring a non-disabled actor (Kevin McHale) to play a character with a disability (Artie). Later episodes attempted to redress this issue by hiring actors with disabilities to portray characters with disabilities.

The producers then capitalized on the popularity of the show and the broader appeal of another genre, reality television, to take this issue one step further. Actors and dancers audition for a spot on *Glee* through *The Glee Project*, a reality television talent contest. They participate in rigorous routines and contestants are progressively eliminated until one person remains and secures a coveted role on *Glee* itself. Several performers with disabilities have participated in each season. The series 1 winner, Blake Jenner, has dyslexia, a feature that became part of the storyline of his *Glee* character Ryan Lynn (The Glee Project Wiki, 2013). Similarly, Ali Stoker, who uses a wheelchair, was cast as a love interest for Artie in another episode (Rizzo, 2013).

The inclusion of people with disabilities is an important diversity initiative and potentially of major benefit to the ageing population who represent a large number of SAG's membership. Disability is constructed as subject to environmental factors, with respondents believing that accommodations would help their employment prospects. Analysis of the survey reveals that these accommodations deal mostly with 'access to food; a nearby bathroom; large print scripts; having the director or production staff speak louder; assistance in walking long distances or climbing stairs; or a place to sit while waiting' (Raynor and Hayward, 2009: 44). However, most respondents were afraid to ask for them:

> 60% never asked for an accommodation because they believed employers would be reluctant to hire them. Many of the performers were unwilling to be candid about their disability in fear of being viewed as an object of pity and incapable of doing the job. (Raynor and Hayward, 2005: 3)

This observation again reflects the legacy of disability stereotypes frequently espoused in the media: that people with disability are objects of pity; that they are lazy; or simply incapable. The media is a difficult industry to break into and television broadcasters are able to select employees from the 'best and the brightest' (Harpe, 1997: 147). And, while *The Glee Project* represents an interesting development, several studies demonstrate that it is rare for actors with disabilities to be cast in roles, even those which portray characters with disabilities (Raynor and Hayward, 2009; Breeden, 2012).

For instance, the 2009 case of a non-disabled actor (Kristian Schmidt) portraying a character with cerebral palsy on the popular Australian drama *Packed to the Rafters* continues the disappointing trend of actors with disabilities being overlooked. The producers of *Packed to the Rafters* believed an actor with cerebral palsy could not keep up with the demands of television production (Knox, 2009). According to Raynor and Haywood, 'no matter what the role, having a disability was not considered an advantage, even when auditioning to play a character with a disability' (2009: 43). Therefore, despite the increase in series regular characters with disabilities on prime time television and the surge of reality television participants with a disability, one estimate suggests that only 1% of regular characters are performed by people with actual disabilities (Breeden, 2012).

Community Media: Towards Disabled Power in the Media?

As we see, despite inclusive rhetoric of some media organizations, governments, policy and industry organizations, there is little reason to believe that goals of access to employment, training, and careers in media industries and professions is a dream on the way to being realized for people with disabilities. In the absence of the openings in mainstream media industries that have – somewhat and very problematically – been afforded other marginalized groups, community television and community projects are one of the few avenues for people with disabilities to gain hands-on training in media production (Harpe, 1997).

With technological change and the widespread availability of cheap digital video, a number of community projects attempted to increase the visibility of people with disabilities in the media during the 1990s. Several of these are outlined in the BBC-produced book *Framed: Interrogating Disability in the Media*. The editors Ann Pointon and Chris Davies argue that a consideration of trends in 'employment and training and the development of a disability arts movement' is crucial to changing the way disability figures in the media: 'it is mainly through this area of activity that expressions of resistance to the dominant 'ablist' ideology and images are being developed' (Pointon and Davies, 1997: 1). Video-making, which has long been used as part of therapy for people with disability, was envisioned to offer the potential of lasting employment for those who became skilled enough (Roberts, 1997). However, in the historical context of art therapy, vocation is rarely the main focus. Often projects are set up with a focus on recreation and making friends rather than learning vocational skills.

One of the difficulties in transforming media work is that initiatives to include people with disability in media industries are often localized and community based and therefore lack the resources and technical expertise required to break into the larger media industry. Nevertheless, a consideration of alternative media is important because they represent a broader social process of mediation and illustrate the uneven distribution of symbolic resources (Couldry, 2002). Public access and community television, for instance, offer important alternatives to mainstream media (Linder, 1999; Rennie, 2006; Forde, 2011). Such communication broadcast media are often seen as existing at the margins of the contemporary media landscape (Ali, 2012) – but actually have long tradition of pride themselves of enjoying wide appeal and achieving significant participation (Howley, 2010). Community television seeks to give voice to community groups such as people with disabilities who might otherwise go unheard.

An example is provided in the case of *No Limits*, a community television programme produced by Disability Media Inc, a Victorian organization, and broadcast on the community television channel spectrum across Australia. *No Limits* seeks to shape a media agenda that recognizes disability beyond the typical clichés of inspirational or tragic hero and give audiences greater exposure to the experience of disability (Smith, 2006). It is a magazine-style programme where a panel of people with disabilities discuss relevant issues. A number of perspectives are offered and the panel often disagree with one another. Their discussions are interspersed with skits that use disability humour to expose disabling social attitudes. Episodes airing throughout the 10th season in 2011, for example, explore a number of issues relevant to people with disability, including dating, sex, media representation, body image, and politics. Community television offers this group of people with disabilities the opportunity to represent disability in a radically different way to mainstream media (King and Mele, 1999: 664).

Thus, public access and community television provide a location for programmes that may not have a large commercial appeal but consider issues relevant to specific community groups. Interestingly, there is little in the fairly well-developed research literature on community, public access, and citizen's media that critically or systematically discusses disability. So we cannot be sure about to what extent community media actually delivers on its own oft-articulated goals and is genuinely accessible to, governed, and controlled by people with disabilities themselves. Given that community media is often lauded for serving as a training ground for volunteers who then go on to careers in mainstream media, there is an additional significance to this issue. Diversity in community and participatory media is an emerging topic, especially in relation to gender and race. But thus far there is nothing of which we are aware that studies disability and community media. So future studies that put community media and disability under the microscope are much needed.

A common thread throughout the industry reports and academic papers cited in this chapter is that access to the media industry is potentially empowering for people with disabilities. While Lori Breeden (Breeden, 2012) finds that community groups of actors with disability offer both personal and social transformation, Peter Dowrick and James Skouge suggest several ways community video projects, community television, and art therapy can empower people with disabilities by giving a voice to the voiceless (Dowrick and Skouge, 2001; Jansen, Pooley and Taub-Pervizpour, 2013). They argue that the creation of an environment which allows people to 'become self-determined beyond the apparent limitations of their circumstances' can result in positive futures for the disability community which has traditionally been characterized by a poor social standing, including low employment.

However, technological change is altering the status of these community activities, with many groups moving online in search of new communities and public spheres. During the 1990s, community-based activists argued that the representation of disability should be reclaimed in an 'irreverent' way through digital video (Hevey, 1997). Although community projects offered this on a small scale – albeit with their political disagreements – informal digital media offers people with disability a broad scale to have their voices heard, their stories told. Similarly, while broadcast television and other media industries are bound within their particular industrial confines, new media platforms are thought to allow uninhibited opportunity for distribution. More significantly for our discussion here, new media are also being widely associated with new possibilities for work and employment. This was ushered spectacularly in the discussions of the 'new economy' in the late 1990s, with accounts abounding of the new kinds of work and workers that were characteristic of websites, web design, and Internet-based enterprises.

There has been a general shift in the nature of work towards the growth of firms and jobs that involve knowledge and information work. There is a growing and significant body of work that analyses and critiques these kinds of claims, focusing on creative and cultural work in particular (Banks, Gill and Taylor, 2013). It is impossible to avoid the need for the discussion of how media work has dramatically changed, especially with the introduction of digital technologies and dramatic changes to traditional media professions such as journalism (Deuze, 2007; Deuze, 2011). These specific changes in media work and professionals compound the general changes, not least the rise of casual, precarious forms of labour. Such changes to work enabled by digital media technologies also involve complex changes to the relationships between public and private spheres, work, and leisure. Various theorists, notably Melissa Gregg, have looked at the gendered nature of these new patterns of intensified, precarious labour infused with digital technology (Gregg, 2011). However, there is no work as yet that thinks through such questions in relation to disability and media – although there are potentially profound implications here. The available studies focus on IT industries and caution that although ushering new opportunities for employment, digital technologies could also create new forms of disablement, particularly with reference to the increasing demands on time (Sapey, 2000). Disability perspectives can actually offer new insights into these shifts in media work and work's new media base; and critical media, cultural, and sociological studies of work offer much to complement traditional work, employment, and rehabilitation perspectives that have dominated research on disability.

Against this backdrop, then, the development of innovative programmes and platforms that take up and engage with new ideas in disability and broadcasting are of significant importance. So we'll now turn to discuss disability-specific websites that produce media and comment on this issue as well.

New Media Technology, Work, and Disability: An Online Paradox

GimpGirl is an online community for women with disabilities that has evolved in response to both the availability and accessibility of new media technologies. *GimpGirl* has also been created in response to members' engagement with the politicization of disability and other aspects of their identities. It began in 1998 as the personal website of founding member Jennifer Cole as a safe place for young women with disabilities transitioning to adulthood (Cole et al., 2011). The community soon progressed to become a listserv and now traverses a number of web 2.0 platforms including Facebook, Livejournal, and Second Life. Indeed *GimpGirl* has been credited with beginning a disability revolution on the Internet. The group hold simultaneous forums across a number of Internet platforms to allow for different accessibility requirements. Discussions on the platforms engage with what Thoreau describes as a 'personal narrative' model of disability to raise consciousness and organize politically (Thoreau, 2006).

User-generated online communities like *GimpGirl* have been credited with paving the way for other disability forums. Public broadcasters in the United Kingdom (BBC) and Australia (ABC) have created online disability media communities through the *Ouch!* and *Ramp Up* platforms, respectively (*Ramp Up* was closed down in May 2014 due to budget cuts). *Ouch!* and *Ramp Up* bring together content from across the media platform of their public broadcasters with op-ed pieces posted by editors and disability writers. Such models of content aggregation around a single portal or platform have been widely used by commercial media organizations – such as magazine and press companies – to create dedicated sites to appeal to women, for instance. In the case of *Ouch!* and *Ramp Up*, they utilize the multimedia platforms to bring a disabled voice to the majority.

In the refrain of this chapter, we don't as yet know much about the characteristics, audiences, and appeal of these kinds of dedicated disability sites. How widely read are they? What are their networks of influence? How often is their material recirculated and picked up by other mainstream as well as alternative media outlets? Are these disability sites read by significant numbers of non-disability-identifying readers? If so, what responses do they have and how do they interpret, and interact with, what they read? And in terms of implications for work, do media professionals with media make a living from producing material for these sites? What are the conditions of labour and implications for their careers in working for *Ouch!* or *Ramp Up*? These are questions addressed to some extent by emerging research on women-focused news initiatives, on gender and newsrooms, and on other areas of media work and professions – but we have no such research as yet that considers such initiatives in relation to disability.

Ahead of such research, we could certainly see the positive implications of these platforms. Although *Ouch!*, in particular, has been criticized for relegating the expert opinion of people with disability to the fringes of media rather than mainstream BBC output (Zajicek, 2007), both encourage grassroots participation of people with and without disability. Through an irreverent tone and disability humour, *Ouch!*, for example, reflects the 'lives and experiences of disabled people' and provides the opportunity to consume images of disability that go beyond tragedy or inspiration narratives. These platforms could also allow people with disabilities to breach the wall – and engage in media production and work that could not only influence mainstream media but also supplant it.

Blogging by People with Disabilities

Blogging is a phenomenon, with its antecedents in the many forms of online communities in the 1980s and 1990s, such as USENET groups, CompuServ email lists, and the bulletin board systems. While early blogs were simply frequently updated personal websites, the emergence of social software to facilitate the updating of blogs without needing to know technical aspects of website management fuelled their rise. The reverse chronological order favoured by this software also made blogs easier to maintain. Blogging is particularly important as it allows people with disabilities the opportunity to value their disability identity and influence the media agenda by offering representation and interpretation from a disability perspective.

Blog writing can influence the media agenda by providing exposure to what would have otherwise been little-known events. Disability blogging recognizes the importance of multiple perspectives on disability. While some disability-specific blogs are predominately concerned with social activism, the genre is varied and encompasses a number of categories, including self-help, parenting of children with a disability, and resources for navigating everyday life with a disability. There are also a number of different blogs specific to the daily experience of different disabilities – something that, as we have noted, has been theorized via the personal narrative model of disability, believed to capture the intersections among the self, society, and the body (Thoreau, 2006). Reflecting upon such a claim, we would observe that although there is social stigma, a physical dimension does exist that influences the experience of disability. Indeed, several disability bloggers see blogging both as a way forward for disability theorization and a way to include and influence the non-disabled population or those with disabilities unaware of the politicization of their identities:

The very eclectic nature of many blogs published by disabled people and our allies has drawn many non-disabled people, as well as disabled people who are less politicized, into the debates. Readers comment that they have had no previous knowledge about or interest in disability, but having enjoyed what we've written about other issues or personal interests, and are learning almost by accident, becoming conscious of the environment, systems and behaviours which disable us. (The Goldfish, 2007)

As discussed in previous chapters, blogging to engage in the conversation regarding media content is a common theme for disability bloggers who wish to challenge negative stereotypes. Disability blogging has the potential to shape a 'new forum for disability advocacy and public engagement' (Kuusisto, 2007). Through the unstructured and open format – a characteristic shared by all blogs – disability blogs allow an image of disability that is absent in mainstream media. Becoming part of the media conversation on disability topics is frequently a motivation for disability bloggers. For example, a blogger who goes by the handle 'Bad Cripple' explains to Beth Haller his reasons for blogging on disability issues: 'My experience with mainstream media has been overwhelmingly negative... I want to be an advocate and antithesis to what the mainstream media is presenting' (Haller, 2010: 3). Bad Cripple sees the potential that a more nuanced view of disability will find its way into mainstream media through his blog. His sentiments are echoed by other disability bloggers who also reflect on the ways people with disabilities have turned to blogging as a way to critique media coverage and offer an alternative point of view. Kay Olson, who blogs under the handle 'Blue', commented:

> I created my blog, The Gimp Parade, as a way to focus and expand on disability issues with an online community of feminist friends ...I wanted to challenge the often ableist thinking of my friends without feeling like my disability identity overwhelmed other aspects of my relationship with that small group of friends. These were friends I'd never met in person. (Olson, 2007)

From this standpoint, blogs encourage conversation and result in different modes of audience engagement. For those in the disability sector, blogging enables a political and social commentary, especially with regard to media representation, stigma, and stereotyping. Blogs can potentially influence the kinds of perspectives heard in the mainstream. Two particular disability news stories debated in blogs – The Ashley X and Terri Schiavo stories – offer insight into the ways people with disability have been both silenced and heard by mainstream media. Blogs influence the political and cultural media agenda and offer people with disabilities new opportunities in the media.

Terry Schiavo, Ashley X and Disability Blogging

As we discussed in Chapter 4, visual and emotional cues and codes are invoked when disability is reported in the news. Disability is 'framed' to offer a familiar narrative. For example, disability is utilized within discussions of voluntary euthanasia to illustrate the contention that you are better off dead than disabled (Haller, 2010). People with disability are usually silenced in these narratives except to provide visual emotional cues to the audience.

In 2005, Terry Schiavo, who had been in a vegetative state since 1990, became the focus of mainstream media attention when the eight-year legal battle regarding the termination of her life support became public. Whereas her husband, Michael Schiavo, wanted to turn off her feeding tube, her parents, Robert and Mary Schindler, maintained that she was conscious and therefore must be kept alive. Media commentary, however, was dominated by bioethicists and 'end of life' experts espousing the dignity of removing her feeding tube (Drake, 2003). Terry Schiavo herself did not have a voice in the debate and some people with disability similarly felt silenced:

Thousands of people with disabilities across the United States are watching the case anxiously. In fact, 12 national disability groups have filed 'friend of the court' briefs in opposition to the efforts to starve Schiavo. Obviously, we want to know how all those commenting in this case feel about the lives of people with Down's syndrome, autism, Alzheimer's and other disabilities. Are they next for death through starvation? It's not so farfetched. (Drake, 2003)

News organizations such as Fox, MSNBC, and CNN accused disability rights organizations of engaging in 'culture wars' (Drake, 2010). Although a disability perspective sought a platform through the friends of the court briefs, this was still in large part disregarded by the mainstream media and repurposed to fit the dominant narrative of better dead than disabled. For example, a CNN article claimed the Schindler's use of the *Americas with Disabilities Act* was 'inapplicable' and contributed to their 'weak argument' about keeping Terry alive (Lazarus, 2005). Terry Schiavo died in March 2005. Olson locates this discussion as a significant juncture in the disability blogosphere, arguing that the way disability issues were covered in the media during this time led some people with disabilities to begin blogging as a way to offer disability perspectives (Olson, 2007).

A contrasting example of societal listening, rather than exclusion, can be found in the case of Ashley X. When an anonymous couple announced on their blog that they had sought hormonal and surgical treatments to ensure their severely disabled daughter (affectionately named Ashley) remain an infant, 'Ashley X' became a major topic in both niche online disability media and the mainstream media. Initially the topic was discussed by people interested in disability on a number of disability blogs. However, as the story grew to gain mainstream audience attention, Google searches and links by mainstream media increased traffic to these little-known disability-specific sites. Many disability bloggers were keen to participate in the conversation and gave mainstream media interviews:

> I was one of a few disability bloggers who linked to early news reports and the initial CNN coverage . . . As incredibly ableist commentary on the case began to infiltrate most every blog discussion that raised the topic, there was considerable pressure to respond with some reasoned disability perspective. (Olson, 2007)

Whereas in the Schiavo case members of the disability community felt silenced and passive, Ashley X represented one of the first times the disability community felt listened to by mainstream media and audiences, despite the intensity of attention regarding the case (Olson, 2007). Although some in the disability blogosphere experienced a 'cruel and malicious backlash' for expressing a different point of view, Olson maintains that the disagreement helped to legitimize disability-informed perspectives in the media. These two stories, although relatively dated now, represent significant milestones in the history of the now well-established disability blogosphere.

In the contrasting case of Terry Schiavo versus Ashley X, we can see the rise of blogging as an especially important way to engage a wide audience concerning disability. The increasing importance of social media has seen the personal narrative model of disability again used for activism and social inclusion. The convergence of these media platforms has raised the disability profile and allowed people previously regarded as 'amateurs', and not part of the official realm of media organizations, outlets, and work, to become widely creditable creators of media. We have very little systematic research on disabled bloggers, and how they fit into, or indeed are transforming, what we take for granted about media work and professions. This kind of inquiry is of course voluminous when it comes to bloggers more generally – in relation to the emergence of citizen journalism, for instance. To take seriously this kind of examination brings us full circle to a persistent question in disability and media – access and formats.

Enabling Media Work: Access and Formats

Significantly, an investigation of disability blogging (Goggin and Noonan, 2006) was included in the first critical study of the ways blogs are used by different groups of people (Bruns and Jacobs, 2006) and emphasized the importance of accessibility and alternative formats. According to Goggin and Noonan, 'the Internet, and blogging in particular, offer new modes for people with disabilities to author, communicate, consume, and exchange in their preferred medium or media' (2006: 166). Goggin and Noonan's focus on customization reveals the continuing importance of blogging to current debates about disability and the media in this regard.

As discussed in Chapter 3, digital technology allows this flexibility, particularly in the current era of personalized devices and software, although in reality this is not always realized. Whether the use of Internet radio and audio blogging by Blind people, or video and sign language blogging by Deaf people, text blogging by people with autism (Davidson, 2008), or many other kinds of blogs that allow for different styles of communication and for disability to be represented in different ways, blogging by people with disabilities has opened up new paradigms of media circulation, exchange, and audience response.

Social media is popularly seen as an important media for people with disability in terms of communication, exchange, and critiquing damaging stereotypes. These sites potentially increase both employment and leisure opportunities for one of the most traditionally isolated groups in society. However, the offline inaccessible environment has, to a certain degree, been replicated online. Many social networking sites are inaccessible to people with a number of impairments. Despite significant advances in accessibility and social attitudes and the recognized benefits of social inclusion for people with disabilities, Hollier notes the continuation of inaccessibility in his report *Sociability: Social Media for People with a Disability*:

> [A]ll of the popular social media tools remain inaccessible to some degree. Facebook, LinkedIn, Twitter, YouTube, blogging websites and the emerging Google+ all feature limited accessibility... Fortunately, users have often found ways around the accessibility barriers such as alternative website portals, mobile apps, additional keyboard navigation shortcuts and online support groups. (Hollier, 2012: 5)

Although Hollier paints a depressing picture, the situation is changing and his report holds much scope for optimism. Comparing the changes from 2008 to 2012, Hollier suggests that people with disabilities are no longer searching for the most accessible social networking site, rather they are looking for ways to access the inaccessible. For example, whereas in 2008 people would ask him *which* was the more accessible social networking site, Facebook or MySpace, people now ask *how* to access Facebook (personal communication). Facebook has established its dominance and people with disabilities don't want to be left out. It is also significant to note that people with disabilities themselves have been integral to the improved accessibility on the YouTube platform (Harrenstien, 2009; Hollier, 2012).

Indeed, ranging from the amateur to the professional, user-generated videos via YouTube in particular have allowed a variety of representation not often seen in mainstream media such as *My Gimpy Life*. Here the putative produsers challenge and update inequitable social tendencies through their amateur media (Bruns and Jacobs, 2006). For example, people with autism (Ellis, 2010b) and people with mental health conditions (Ellis, 2012b) are particularly active on YouTube using the platform for community creation and alternative media representations. Whereas the mainstream media has been accused of adopting a disabling agenda when it comes to representing disability (Barnes, 1992; Hevey, 1997; Nelson, 2000), social media video platforms such as YouTube have been recognized for their educative potential regarding disability awareness (Wollheim, 2007; Columna et al., 2009; Ellis, 2010b).

Since Hollier's 2012 accessibility review, YouTube has introduced further improvements to access with their own integrated captioning editor.

In contrast to YouTube, Facebook represents somewhat of a paradox in the discussion of disability, new media, and media access. Like YouTube, Facebook was awarded only one star in the AbilityNet's 2008 accessibility review. However, Facebook has also allowed people with disability to be included in political interest and comment (Haller, 2010). Take the case of *The Official Petition for a More Accessible Facebook*, which utilized Facebook's group function to highlight the issue of Facebook's poor accessibility for people with vision impairment and learning disabilities.

The group was started by Andrew McKay, a student with vision impairment, and called on Facebook to rectify seven accessibility issues he identified in consultation with other group members (McKay, 2007). The petition garnered thousands of supporters, international attention, and eventually led to an accessibility overhaul of the entire site in consultation with the American Foundation for the Blind (AFB) (Ellis and Kent, 2011). The AFB, who also launched action against Facebook using the Facebook interface, described their interactions with Facebook as responsive to finding solutions to accessibility problems (Augusto, 2009). From being described as falling well below basic accessibility compliance (AbilityNet, 2008), following its AFB accessibility overhaul Facebook was touted as 'good choice for people with disabilities' (Cahill and Hollier, 2009). This retrofit would not have taken place if not for the activist intervention of people with disabilities, ironically on Facebook – though accessibility issues remain.

As a text-based medium, competitor platform Twitter should render people with disabilities, and those without, equal. However, Twitter has been criticized for its poor level of accessibility (Cahill, 2009), and, disappointingly, it has no accessibility policy. In fact, Twitter received an accessibility rating of 0% in 2012 because 'every element on the website [has] accessibility issues' (Hollier, 2012). However, there is some encouraging news. Twitter encourages users to access it using third-party applications and a number of accessible versions have been innovated by third parties to compensate for the inaccessibility of Twitter itself. For example, the accessible Twitter platform Easy Chirp grew out of Twitter's ethos of innovation and was created by Dennis Lembree, a web developer active in the Twitter accessibility community.

Conclusion

The need to reform media institutions and professions has, of course, also been a theme of discussions of how women, racialized, and other marginalized groups are portrayed. Discussions in the context of disability continue key themes such as increasing levels of employment to allow disability voices to be heard at every level. Against the background of unenforceable media guidelines, community media has offered a rare opportunity for new public spheres. Yet we know little about how well community media, which prides itself on inclusiveness and advancing access, actually delivers this for aspiring volunteers and future media workers keen to gain experiences.

While debates regarding employment and access continue and nominal progress is made, blogs, YouTube, Facebook, and Twitter provide valuable real time opportunity for people with disability to engage in media industries and shape the media agenda. Blogging by people with disabilities has opened up new paradigms of media circulation, exchange, and audience response. Blogging has allowed people with disability to be included in political interest and comment. Along with mitigating various types of impairments through alternative formats, blogs are inclusive of the disability rights agenda. The new forms of televisual culture – centring on YouTube and other video-sharing and distribution platforms – allow 'ordinary' people with disabilities to present videos and programmes on their lives, as well as presenting a new kind of medium where non-traditional media actors (disability or human rights groups, for instance) can quite easily devise and circulate media content. Similarly, social media – through the vogue applications of Facebook and Twitter – have not only been at the heart of reshaping of media, they also allow disability to figure in media in distinctive and novel ways. As we have discussed, it is disappointing that these new, much vaunted social media platforms have often been tardy and resistant to innovation in accessibility. Such ongoing design dynamics concerning accessibility are crucial if these new platforms are to deliver much-needed opportunity for a broadening of users to make, produce, and circulate media. This helps to pave the way for people with disabilities to be finally able to transform media work, and thus powerfully reshape old and new media systems.

7 Conclusion: Doing Justice to Disability and Media

In July 2010, disabled documentary filmmaker Billy Golfus appeared on a new YouTube channel 'Its Our Story Project'. The channel's stated goal was to 'make disability history national and accessible' by interviewing key Americans with disabilities. Golfus issued a scathing attack on the lack of opportunity afforded to him in the media industry, despite being an Emmy-nominated filmmaker for his 1995 documentary *When Billy Broke His Head... and Other Tales of Wonder*. Seeing industry prejudice against him as a person with a disability as a major hurdle to a career in the media, Golfus describes the way people interacted with him as opposed to his non-disabled co-director David Simpson during the making of *When Billy Broke His Head*:

> I was constantly being treated like the down person, as the disabled person always is in a number of contexts. Instead of being treated like a mensch, you know? And so I was constantly being the one that was talked to through someone... I wrote it, I was Emmy nominated for it. For the script. Those were your true words coming through on the film... It wasn't his film. It was my friends. It was my disability and he got the career. He got to work at PBS. (Golfus, 2010)

Golfus maintains that, despite being the key driver of a film that received wide critical acclaim, he was silenced in his professional interactions and aspirations. Golfus' critique raises several key issues regarding disability and the media that we are concerned with in this book. His experience reflects the social, attitudinal, and institutional disablement people with disability experience when trying to enter media industries. In telling this 'behind the scenes' story, Golfus also highlights the ways disability is used by the media to tell stories, sell papers, and keep audiences watching. Thus, representation and participation are central to our investigation of disability and the media. Golfus' experience and critique provides a reminder of the stakes for people with disabilities in the media.

Throughout this book, we have tried to show the ways disability is highly significant for the media. The media is ubiquitous; it plays a significantly heightened role in both daily private and public life. As the significance of this role increases, so too do the costs of being excluded from it. As we have shown throughout this book and Golfus reiterates here, people with disability are excluded from the media, both through limiting representations and the lack of opportunity to participate in the production cycle. In addition, the accessibility of media for many people with disability is a key issue, which is now required by international law.

The adequacy of media to do justice to the full range of groups and individuals in society is an enduring theme. While we are more familiar with scrutinizing and exploring the media from standpoints of gender, sexuality, race, or geopolitical power struggles, disability is a relatively new entrant as a key concern in media, but once recognized it presents considerable challenges with very rich possibilities and openings too. Long-standing questions of the role and responsibility of the media to provide balance, objectivity, accurate information, and adequate narratives and imagination for democratic societies can be enhanced by considering disability.

What is not widely realized about disability is something we have sought to explain in this book. Disability is not just those 'poor people', tragic and inspirational victims by turns, who are very 'special', and need dedicated (read hardly-ever-watched-or-read-or-listened-to) genres of the media. Disability is not about providing an opportunity to demonstrate the triumph of the human spirit, and how selfless and charitable we can be, if we only tried hard enough. Disability does touch each of us. Whether we identify with disability, or not, if we live long enough, as the refrain goes, we will all experience significant impairment and even the social depreciation, malalignment, marginalization, exclusion, and oppression that are the deep cultural and political dimensions of disability.

It is not a stretch to suggest that, in defining disability, we are defining what it is to be human as well as what is considered non-human. Further still, as the dark histories of religious thought and practice in faith communities show, our ideas of the spiritual are profoundly shaped by disability. So disability is a key concern in media, but it profoundly shapes what media is, what it does, who works in media and benefits from it, and who gets to use media for what purposes, with what consequences.

In this concluding chapter we will bring together the main arguments and insights of this book, and outline some of the tough challenges – as well as extraordinary opportunities – that flow from a critical understanding of disability as integral to media.

A 360-Degree View on Disability and Media

Typically the way that disability has tended to crop up in media studies, policy, and practice has been to do with access. Many of the communications, media, and new media studies conferences and research literature we have encountered since the early 1990s have often had a small number of presentations or studies of disability accessibility. This is especially true with the advent of the World Wide Web, where, as we have discussed, accessibility became an important issue, which finally saw disability registered as a serious concern – at least when it came to one element of the Internet. Amazingly, though, as we have explained, despite the rise of very significant intellectual, political, and cultural movements to do with other integral yet 'othered' aspects of society, which were taken up in media, communication, and cultural studies and disciplines like sociology, history, anthropology and others, engagement with critical accounts of disability has remained too much of a minority affair.

We have to confess we are baffled why there is such a gulf concerning disability when it comes to the study of media. Useful work has been done in many areas, which we have sought to acknowledge and draw attention to here. Importantly, disabled academics have strongly and consistently participated in critiques of media and disability. To be sure, we do have a few ideas why disability is a deficit (in many senses), a topic still infrequently incorporated into media and journalism courses or rarely raised as a central topic in discussions of communication.

As we make clear, we see disability as including in an indivisible (if not well-theorized) way: accessibility, representation, social participation, economics, media industries, work, and leisure. In short, if much of the history of media studies, in particular, has been about finding the ways to connect enquiries into political economy and policy with questions of signs, meaning, cultural texts, practices, and value, then to join such discussions with grounded understandings of audiences and trace the connections between media and politics, then it's time for disability to get the party started!

Hopefully, we have helped to do so by indicating some of the ways we think that media studies can illuminate the contemporary dynamics of society, in which disability is now recognized as so important.

And, in return, we have tried to reread and rethink media – the circuits, communicative architectures, forms, formats, channels, platforms, and technologies so central to our futures – via a long overdue perspective from disability experiences, theories, and research.

The Party's Over . . . Let the New Party Begin

What we argue strongly, following feminist, critical race, post-colonial, queer, and other media thinkers, is that band-aid solutions just won't cut it. Hence, our media theory of disability (and, vice versa, our disability theory of media) encompasses accessibility, representation, consumption and production, media making, and media work. Thankfully, it's now a great time for us, as media students, teachers, professionals, and policymakers, to build on the important research, media production, and debates over the past three decades and undertake the vast work still needed.

For one thing, although useful in shaping different images of disability, guidelines are nothing if not context specific, and unsurprisingly there is little consensus on these images, apart from the broad injunction to avoid patronizing and discriminatory language. For example, in the country we live in – Australia – there are at least seven major guidelines dispersed among eight states and territories. Most importantly, as we have sought to explain, guidelines are just that: a prompt to memory, a shorthand, and, most of all, a starting and jumping off point, for unleashing all the professional acumen and creativity that journalists and news producers are renowned for – in order to do justice to representing disability accurately and adequately, and wooing audiences, and making good business sense in doing so.

When it comes to positive images of disability, who could now argue against these? Apart from the spleen-venting rants to be found on social media platforms and mostly now concealed and not disclosed in everyday life, to argue against positive images on disability would be like decrying parenthood. Celebrations of disability have proven especially popular for large-scale 'watercooler', nation-binding events, such as the Paralympics. However these images, as we have noted, often do not reflect the interests and experiences of the very diverse range of people with disability, and still too often rely upon the cherished stereotypes and disabling images and attitudes that are now being challenged.

So, we wonder if one of the new directions to transform disability and the media, and through this contribute to the embrace of disability in society, is through encouraging creativity, experiments, courageous thinking, saying the un-sayable, and the various other tools by which societies have reimagined themselves in order to effect much-needed transformation. Let's take a risk... Actually, much of the media – to hazard an indefensible generalization, given the range of branches of media there are – have been spectacularly *crap* in doing justice to disability. We use this technical term in a spirit of hyperbole and exasperation, but there is quite some evidence to back up the argument that it is so.

Laurels have been rested in taking initiatives such as guidelines for journalists. The odd disability action plan or programme has been initiated, often without sufficient resources, evaluation, or accountability. Broadcasters, especially public service media, have congratulated themselves on commissioning one or two celebrated series on disability, which even include actors with disabilities. By exception, people with disabilities find careers in media and are lauded – at least some of the time. Many media technology companies, even in funky new digital media, have to be dragged kicking and screaming into making their networks, products, and services accessible. Around the world, media regulators, by and large, did so little until the mid-to-late 1990s to articulate and protect disability as part of their broader mandates (public interest, for instance), that it beggared belief. Governments were reluctant to enact adequate legislative change to address disability aspects of media until legal action was threatened and taken, and lobbying and advocacy was taken in earnest and, then, until the UN Convention on the Rights of Persons with Disabilities was signed. In the main, media education and training institutions have little track record, as yet, of using their strategically important role to leverage more opportunities for people with disabilities to enter and gain good careers in media professions. For our part, as media academics, we have been slow to extend the kind of critical attention, teaching, and research to disability which has been underway for a long time with other comparable topics. Yet disability is a fundamental aspect of the social, and a consideration of disability offers an opportunity to think through the implications of the pervasive role media plays in our everyday lives.

Ironically, it has often been other domains than media which have generated new visions, vocabularies, and vehicles for imagining disability differently: dance, poetry, literature and writing, comedy, accessible arts, activism, music, and cinema. Powerful new ideas about disability have come from sources other than traditional press, magazines, broadcasting, advertising, or even new media forms such as the Internet, mobiles, or computer games. One case in point we mentioned is disability, comedy, and humour. Another is the renaissance of disability culture and art that made the London Paralympics so groundbreaking, and in doing so forced media to expand its mental, attitudinal, and production bandwidth to cope. Of course, this is a perilous generalization to make, but if there is a grain of truth in it, then it should spur us to ensure media catch up with disability, its cultural potency, and social innovation.

Media Making a Real Difference

It is of real concern that people with disability may not have access to either the media or the information provided through specific avenues. This is especially the case given that media work in much different ways now than they did previously. Disability is communicated in particular ways via the affordances, characteristics, and cultures of use associated with specific platforms.

To take just one example, natural disaster alerts communicated via social media, the implications for people unable to access these platforms are potentially deadly (Kent and Ellis, 2013). Digital television access is important, as Lauren Henley, advocacy and policy officer for Australian organization Blind Citizens Australia, explains:

> You might think that missing out on television is no great loss, but it's about more than watching the latest episode of *Days of our Lives*. Like the rest of my friends and family, I want to have choice about what I watch and have the ability to be informed about what is going on in the world. I lost many things when I lost my sight, but one of the things that I lost was social inclusion; a term that is often thrown around but rarely clearly defined. (Henley, 2012)

As Henley makes plain, it's pretty simple really. People with disability, like their friends and family, want a choice in what they watch, and the ability to be informed about what was going on in the world. As we discussed in Chapter 3, new platforms such as digital television stand to play an important role here. In addition to the audio descriptions Henley and other Blind consumers might use, digital television has the capability to provide features for people with disability, such as captions, lip-reading avatars, signing avatars, spoken subtitles, and 'clean' audio.

Although new forms of disability have been created through new media, so too have disability-specific media practices. These have been accompanied by troubling contradictions. For instance, the introduction of new media has opened up new modes of communication, yet aggressive market forces have disregarded the importance of accessibility in mainstream areas. For example, Facebook has had a vexed relationship with accessibility since its release to the wider public in 2004. It has been described as totally inaccessible to people with vision impairments and intellectual disability (McKay, 2007), undergone an accessibility overhaul under the direction of the American Foundation for the Blind (Ellis, 2011), and been described as a 'good choice' for people with disability (Cahill and Hollier, 2009). More recently, social media experts noted inaccessible features creeping back into the site's design and encouraged disabled users to access the site through mobile apps and form communities of experts who could share knowledge about accessible work around (Hollier, 2012). Finally, in a very welcome move, Facebook has introduced a dedicated accessibility team (Hollier, 2013).

As media is 'not just another business', as the catch-cry goes, but is central to social life, the time is long overdue for transformation of disabling arrangements. And the handy thing is such changes stand to benefit everyone. If you design for disability, the saying goes, you design for everyone. Making the local train station accessible via a lift (rather than forcing everyone to use stairs) means that parents with infants in prams and strollers, commuters carrying large parcels, or those of us who are tired or have mobility issues can get better access and better service. In the media, disability design and access concerns intersect with the needs of the non-disabled population who also seek usable, easy-to-understand, customized, and individualized technology as a matter of course. Research suggests that if people with disability find technology difficult to use, so too would the majority of consumers. Taking up that notion, the UK Office of Communications advised companies to develop products with people with disability in mind, to gain the maximum usability (Sinclair et al., 2007). Accessibility and usability of media products, services, and technologies often raise difficult questions of design, information, policy, and cost. But grappling with accessibility remains a key issue for disability media reform.

Representation

A very interesting feature of contemporary media that we have explored in this book is its representation of disability and the attempts made to redress the lack of representation of people with disability. We looked at quite a few examples across news and television drama, crime, and reality genres at the ways that disability is represented. In presenting our analysis and views, we have been conscious that there are many other possible readings and perspectives on what these texts, images, and programmes mean. So we hope that our explanation of concepts and provision of examples of disability reading of media has opened up new avenues for you to explore this. Of course, disability is a great topic for student assignments, but critical analysis, conversation, and debates about how disability figures in media is a really important resource for opening up broader debate and stimulating needed change in disability in society generally.

In discussing representation of disability, we have noted that many media theorists believe that we need to move beyond the impasse of representation. Moreover, while scholars point out that not everything related to media has to do with representation, there are those who raise other questions. One fertile avenue for thinking beyond otherness has to do with acknowledgement and working through the complexity of speaking and voice and listening in media. A diverse group of scholars has called for an acknowledgement of the importance of listening to the dynamics of culture in which media plays a decisive role (O'Donnell, Lloyd and Dreher, 2009). Broadly speaking, the 'listening' turn aims to be a corrective that acknowledges that it is not sufficient for previously marginalized, excluded, or overlooked groups to be accorded the formal right to speak, or even to be able to practically achieve this. Rather, speaking occurs in a relationship of listening, where listening is premised on recognition (Fraser, 1995; Honneth, 2001) and involves dedicated labour and resources. In media, of course, the notion of listening brings back into the view the audience, as well as the importance it plays in completing the meaning-making. Indeed, disability has very interesting things to add to this important rethinking of the politics of voice and to our societal arrangements concerning listening: who listens, how do they do so, and what comes of it (Goggin, 2009).

Delivering on Promises of Media and Social Participation

British disability theorists David Hevey (1997) and Colin Barnes (1992) long ago identified the power of the media and its tendency to frame as a reason to include people with disabilities in the media production cycle. As we discuss, people with disabilities remain under-represented as workers in the media industry. In the meantime, it is so-called user-generated content on YouTube, Facebook, Twitter, and blogs as well as official and unofficial forums that is becoming the route to opportunity for participation, distribution, and exchange for people with disabilities in media. Significantly, as we have discussed throughout this book, a number of useful online disability networks have been established online by organizations, academic networks, and individuals such as Beth Haller's Media dis&dat, the University of Leeds' Disability Studies Archive, Temple University's Disability Studies blog carnivals, the BBC's *Ouch!*, and a large number of individual bloggers and Twitter users. In addition to increasing the disability media profile, some of this user-generated content has even influenced the mainstream media on some occasions.

In order to remain competitive in a rapidly changing media environment, television for example has had to adapt, utilizing and innovating various formats and genres as well as methods of broadcast. Producers are utilizing social media as a method to leverage audiences. For example, when Oprah Winfrey launched her OWN channel, she put an open call for auditions for people to host their own shows. Twenty-six-year-old Zach Anner, who has cerebral palsy, posted a video to Oprah.com pitching a comedic travel show. His audition video received 9 million votes and his six-part travel series *Rolling with Zach* eventually appeared on OWN.

Zach's audition video subverted the usual inspiration/tragedy narratives of disability on television through disability humour. He sought to highlight a common accessibility issue people with disability regularly experience – travelling. In a funny and self-depreciating audition, Zach describes himself as having cerebral palsy or 'the sexiest of the palsys'. He demonstrates that while he is not suited to a cooking show ('next lesson: how to cook takeout') or health and lifestyle ('this isn't yoga, this is me putting on my pants, America doesn't want to see that') he would be the perfect candidate to make a travel show. Throughout his audition Zach highlights, rather than hides, the unusual way his body moves to gain audience rapport. As an instance of the working across multiple media platforms that Henry Jenkins theorizes in his 2006 book *Convergence Culture* (Jenkins, 2006), Zach's audition video offers a radical representation of disability that is rarely seen on mainstream media.

Perhaps the shift to participatory media cultures will provide people with disabilities an opportunity to bring the non-disabled world to it. We are seeing some evidence of this in the way that people with disabilities are using new media platforms to tell new stories, or perhaps tell old stories in a new way, outside of the confines of the media world. Take, for example, *The Specials*, a web series about five young adults with intellectual disabilities who live in a share house in Brighton, the United Kingdom. *The Specials* has been positively reviewed and described as '[shining] a light on a subculture usually confined to special-ed classes and specialized institutions' (Shaw, 2010).

The Internet series is an important forum, particularly for the alternative representation of disability that it offers. Like many soap opera subgenres of television, the first series ended on a love triangle between Sam, Megan, and Lewis with every other housemate offering their own perspective on who Megan should choose and the appropriateness of her behaviour. In late 2011, the creators of *The Specials* – Katy and Dan Lock – announced that the second season would be delayed because the programme was to be shown on network television in the United States, leaving fans hanging as to what actually happened between Sam, Megan, and Lewis. At the time of writing, although it has been announced that it will air on OWN, *The Specials* has not yet aired. So it's unclear about key questions: will the first season be 're-edited' for network television? Will the subculture *The Specials* inhabits be accurately portrayed or will these multifaceted characters be repurposed to fit the television stereotypes that this web series deviates from? Will the audience 'listen' to this new image of disability or will tragedy/inspiration discourse of interpretation dominate?

In the case of Zach, just mentioned, when he became officially aligned with Oprah he was repackaged from having the 'sexiest of all the palsys' on his audition video to being 'wheelchair-bound'; courtesy of his biography on Oprah's website:

Wheelchair-bound lady magnet Zach, discusses his many talents and idea for a TV show designed to inspire people who never thought they could travel. Join Zach as he globe-trots to some of the most notoriously inaccessible locations and embraces the spontaneous nature of world travel! No matter what the obstacle, he'll face every bump in the road with a smile. (Winfrey, 2012)

This description of Zach as wheelchair-bound is highly problematic and, as we discussed in Chapter 3, contravenes guidelines regarding reporting on disability. Wheelchairs do not confine people, inaccessible wheelchair locations do. In addition, through his association with Oprah and her vast resources in the media world Zach would be able to navigate inaccessible locations with an ease not available to ordinary people with disabilities.

So although the media world may continue to produce a vision of society and offer it for consumption, with the affordances of user-generated content, users are able to become more active in the production of media messages. As people with disability engage in both the productive and consumptive activities of online media, they help shape a shared understanding of disability issues. Whether such new media cultures and platforms can be the fulcrum for the profound transformation needed in disability and media – and a much broader notion of participation also – is a question of great consequence.

Bibliography

@Uncle_A_Trotter (2013) 'Miley Cyrus Has Hired 7 Dwarves as Backing Dancers – They Whistle as They Twerk', *Twitter*, 17 September. Available at https://twitter.com/Uncle_A_Trotter/status/379896105640534016

Abbott, S. (ed.) (2010) *The Cult TV Book* (London and New York: I.B. Tauris).

AbilityNet (2008) *State of the eNation Web Accessibility Reports: Social Networking websites.* Available at http://www.abilitynet.org.uk/docs/enation/2008SocialNetworkingSites.pdf

Abou-Zahra, S., J. Brewer and S. L. Henry (2013) 'Essential Components of Mobile Web Accessibility', W4A 13 Proceedings of the 10th International Cross-Disciplinary Conference on Web Accessibility, article no. 5, 13–17 May, Rio de Janeiro, Brazil.

Abruzzese, A., N. Barile, J. Gebhardt, J. Vincent and L. Fortunati (eds) (2012) *The New Television Ecosystem* (New York: Peter Lang).

Anderson, B. (1983) *Imagined Communities: Reflections on the Origin and Spread of Nationalism* (London: Verso).

Accessible Media Inc (AMI) (2014) 'About AMI', Accessible Media Inc. Available at http://www.ami.ca/about/Pages/default.aspx

Ali, C. (2012) 'Media at the Margins: Policy and Practice in American, Canadian and British Community Television', *International Journal Communication* vol. 6, pp. 1119–1138.

Alper, M., E. Ellcessor, K. Ellis and G. Goggin (2015) 'Reimagining the Good Life with Disability: Communication, New Technology, and Humane Connections', in H. Wang (ed.) *Communication and the Good Life* (New York: Peter Lang).

Anderson, P. J., G. Ogola and M. Williams (eds) (2014) *The Future of Quality News Journalism: A Cross-Continental Analysis* (New York: Routledge).

Ang, I. (1991) *Desperately Seeking the Audience* (London: Routledge).

Anner, Z. (2012) 'Zach's Oprah Audition', *YouTube*, 14 June. Available at https://www.youtube.com/watch?v=T_35KKa3b1c

Armbrust, R. (2005) 'Bias High Against Disabilities', *Back Stage* 28 July–3 August, p. 3.

Augusto, C. R. (2009) 'Making Facebook Accessible for Everyone', *The Facebook Blog*, 7 April. Available at https://www.facebook.com/notes/facebook/making-facebook-accessible-for-everyone/71852922130

Auslander, G. and N. Gold (1999) 'Disability Terminology in the Media: A Comparison of Newspaper Reports in Canada and Israel', *Social Science & Medicine* vol. 48, pp. 1395–1405.

Australian Communications and Media Authority (ACMA) (2010) *Digital Radio Accessibility: Developments with Digital Radio Technology for People with Disabilities* (Sydney: ACMA). Available at http://www.acma.gov.au/Industry/Broadcast/Spectrum-for-broadcasting/Broadcast-planning/digital-radio-1

Baldwin, S. C. (1993) *Pictures in the Air: The Story of the National Theatre of the Deaf* (Washington, DC: Gaulladet University Press).

Banks, M., R. Gill and S. Taylor (eds) (2013) *Theorizing Cultural Work: Labour, Continuity and Change in the Creative Industries* (New York: Routledge).

Barnes, C. (1992) *Disabling Imagery and the Media: An Exploration of the Principles for Media Representations of Disabled People*. Available at http://www.leeds.ac.uk/disability-studies/archiveuk/Barnes/disabling%20imagery.pdf.

Barnes, C. and G. Mercer (2005) 'Disability, Work, and Welfare: Challenging the Social Exclusion of Disabled People', *Work Employment & Society* vol. 19, pp. 527–545.

Barnes, C. and G. Mercer (2010) *Exploring Disability: A Sociological Introduction*, 2nd ed. (Cambridge and Malden, MA: Polity).

Barnes, C., M. Oliver and L. Barton (eds) (2002) *Disability Studies Today* (Cambridge and Malden, MA: Polity).

Barlett, J., S. Black and M. Northen (eds) (2011) *Beauty is a Verb: The New Poetry of Disability* (El Paso, TX: Cinco Puntos).

Barthes, R. (1973) *Mythologies*, trans. A. Laver (St Albans: Paladin).

Bauman, H.-D. L., H. M. Rose and J. L. Nelson (eds) (2006) *Signing the Body Poetic: Essays on American Sign Language Literature* (Berkeley, CA: University of California Press).

Ben-Moshea, L. and J. J. W. Powell (2007) 'Sign of Our Times? Revis(it)ing the International Symbol of Access', *Disability & Society* vol. 22, pp. 489–505.

Bennett, J. and T. Brown (eds) (2008) *Film and Television after DVD* (New York: Routledge).

Berlant, L. (2008) *The Female Complaint: The Unfinished Business of Sentimentality in American Culture* (Durham, NC: Duke University Press).

Blake, R. and J. Stevens (2004) *Adjusting the Picture: a Producer's Guide to Disability* (London: Disability Rights Commission, Employer's Forum on Disability, and Independent Television Network). Available at http://www.ofcom.org.uk/static/archive/itc/uploads/Adjusting_the_Picture.pdf

Blanck, P. (2015) *eQuality: The Struggle for Web Accessibility by Persons with Cognitive Disabilities* (Cambridge: Cambridge University Press).

Blood, R. W., P. Putnis and J. Pirkis (2002) 'Mental-Illness News as Violence', *Australian Journal of Communication* vol. 29, pp. 59–82.

Blumberg, A. (2013) 'Miley Cyrus Backup Dancer, Hollis Jane, Speaks Out Against "Degrading" VMA Performance,' *Huffington Post*, 10 November 2013. Available at http://www.huffingtonpost.com/2013/10/11/miley-cyrus-backup-dancer_n_4085057.html

Bobbit, R. (2010) *Us against Them: The Political Culture of Talk Radio* (Plymouth: Lexington).

Bogdan, R. (1990) *Freak show: Presenting Human Oddities for Amusement and Profit* (Chicago, IL: University of Chicago Press).

Bolt, D. (ed.) (2014) *Changing Social Attitudes Toward Disability: Perspectives from Historical, Cultural, and Educational Studies* (New York: Routledge).

Boltanski, L. (1999) *Distant Suffering: Morality, Media and Politics*, trans. G. Burchell (Cambridge: Cambridge University Press).

Bosse, I. (2006) *Behinderung im Fernsehen* (Wiesbaden: Deutscher Universitäts-Verlag).

De Botton, A. (2014) *The News: A User Manual* (London: Penguin).

Boudreu, D. (2012) 'Social Media Accessibility: Where are We Today?', Presentation to CSUN 2012, San Diego, 1 March. Available at http://www.slideshare.net/AccessibiliteWeb/20120301-web041socialmedia

Boyd-Barrett, O. (ed.) (2010) *News Agencies in the Turbulent Era of the Internet* (Barcelona: Generalitat de Catalunya).

Boyd-Barrett, O. and T. Rantanen (eds) (1998) *The Globalization of News* (London and Thousand Oaks, CA: Sage).

Boyle, R. and R. Haynes (2009) *Power Play: Sport, The Media and Popular Culture* (Edinburgh: Edinburgh University Press).

Breeden, L. (2012) 'Transformative Occupation in Practice: Changing Media Images and Lives of People with Disabilities,' *Occupation, Participation and Health* vol. 32, pp. S15–S24.

Briggs, C. (2013) 'OMG at the MTV VMA's!' *Stay at Home Mum*, 8 September. Available at http://www.stayathomemum.com.au/my-kids/omg-at-the-mtv-vmas/

Brisenden, S. (1986) 'Independent Living and the Medical Model of Disability', *Disability, Handicap & Society* vol.1, no. 2, pp. 173–178.

Brooks, D., M. Campbell, M. Connolly, N. Heyer and N. Fintham (2012) *Creative Skillset Employment Census of the Creative Media Industries* (London: Creative Skillset). Available at http://courses.creativeskillset.org/assets/0000/2819/Census_report_6.pdf.

Brueggemann, B. (2007) 'On (Almost) Passing,' *College English* vol. 59, pp. 647–660.

Bruns, A. and J. Jacobs (eds) (2006) *Uses of Blogs* (New York: Peter Lang).

Brunsdon, C. and D. Morley (1978) *Everyday Television: Nationwide* (London: BFI).

Buchanan, R. (1999) 'The Silent Worker and the Building of a Deaf Community, 1890–1929', in J. V. Van Cleve (ed.), *Deaf History Unveiled: Interpretations from the New Scholarship* (Washington, DC: Gaulladet University Press), pp. 172–197.

Butler, P., M. Taylor and J. Ball (2013) 'Welfare Cuts will Cost Disabled People £28bn Over 5 years', *Guardian*, 27 March, http://www.theguardian.com/society/2013/mar/27/welfare-cuts-disabled-people

Burns, S. (2010) 'Words Matter: Journalists, Educators, Media Guidelines and Representation of Disability', *Asia Pacific Media Educator* vol. 20, pp. 277–284.

Butson, T. (2009) 'Fearnley Fury at Wheelchair Humiliation in Airport', *The Age* (Melbourne), 24 November. Available at http://www.theage.com.au/travel/ travel-news/fearnley-fury-at-wheelchair-humiliation-in-airport-20091124-j99a.html

Cahill, M. (2009) 'A Wake-Up Call For Twitter', *New Matilda*, 1 December. Available at https://newmatilda.com/2009/12/01/wake-call-twitter

Cahill, M. and S. Hollier (2009) *Social Media Accessibility Review – Version 1.0* (Sydney: *Media Access Australia*). Available at http://mediaaccess.org.au/sites/ default/files/files/Social%20Media%20Accessibility%20Review%20v1_0.pdf

Campbell, F. (2009) *Contours of Ableism: The Production of Disability and Abledness* (London: Palgrave Macmillan).

Cavanagh, R., L. Krstic and N. Steele (2005) *The Presence, Portrayal and Participation of Persons with Disabilities on Television Programming: A Research Report Presented to the Canadian Association of Broadcasters* (Manotic, ON: Connectus). Available at http://www.cab-acr.ca/english/research/05/sub_sep1605_research.htm.

Chadwick, A. (2013) *The Hybrid Media System: Politics and Power* (Oxford: Oxford University Press).

Cheu, J. (ed.) (2013) *Diversity in Disney Films: Critical Essays on Race, Ethnicity, Gender, Sexuality and Disability* (Jefferson, NC: McFarland & Co).

Chivers, S. (2011) *The Silvering Screen: Old Age and Disability in Cinema* (Toronto, ON: University of Toronto Press).

Chivers, S. and N. Markotić (ed.) (2010) *The Problem Body: Projecting Disability on Film* (Columbus, OH: Ohio State University Press).

Clarke, M. J. (2012) *Transmedia Television: New Trends in Network Serial Production* (New York: Continuum).

Cole, J., J. Nolan, Y. Seko, K. Mancuso and A. Ospina (2011) 'GimpGirl Grows Up: Women with Disabilities Rethinking, Redefining, and Reclaiming Community', *New Media & Society* vol. 13, pp. 1161–1179.

Coleman, S. and K. Ross (2010) *The Media and the Public: 'Them' and 'Us' in Media Discourse* (Malden, MA and Chichester: Wiley).

Columna, L., K. Arndt, L. Lieberman and S. Yang (2009) 'Using Online Videos for Disability Awareness', *Journal of Physical Education, Recreation & Dance* vol. 80, pp. 19–24.

Corker, M. (1996) *Deaf Transitions: Images and Origins of Deaf Families, Deaf Communities, and Deaf Identities* (London: Jessica Kingsley)

Corker, M. (1998) *Deaf and Disabled or Deafness Disabled?: Towards a Human Rights Perspective* (Buckingham and Philadelphia, PA: Open University Press).

Corker, M. (2000) 'Disability Politics, Language Planning and Inclusive Social Policy', *Disability & Society* vol. 15, no. 3, pp. 445–462.

Corker, M. and T. Shakespeare (eds) (2002) *Disability/Postmodernity: Embodying Disability Theory* (London: Continuum).

Couch, A. (2013) 'How FX's "Legit" Became the Darling of the Disabled Community', *The Hollywood Reporter*, 22 March. Available at http://www. hollywoodreporter.com/live-feed/fxs-legit-jim-jefferies-embraced-430325

Couldry, N. (2002) 'Mediation and Alternative Media, or Relocating the Centre of Media and Communication Studies', *Media International Australia* no. 103, pp. 24–31.

Couldry, N., A. Hepp and F. Krotz. (eds) (2010) *Media Events in a Global Age* (New York: Routledge).

Creed, B. (2003) *Media Matrix: Sexing the New Reality* (Sydney: Allen & Unwin).

Crisell, A. (1994) *Understanding Radio* (London: Routledge).

Cumberbatch, G. and R. Negrine (1992) *Images of Disability on Television* (London: Routledge).

Curtin, M., J. Holt and K. Sanson (eds) (2014) *Distribution Revolution: Conversations about the Digital Future of Film and Television* (Oakland, CA: University of California Press).

Cyrus, M. (2013) 'MC & the Boos', *Twitter*, 8 September. Available at pic.twitter.com/QhnMVuE5JJ

Dakroury, A., M. Eid, Y. R. Kamalipour (eds) (2009) *The Right to Communicate: Historical Hopes, Global Debates and Future Premises* (Dubuque, IA: Kendall Hunt).

Dant, T. (2012) *Television and the Moral Imaginary: Society through the Small Screen* (Basingstoke: Palgrave Macmillan).

Darke, P. (2004) 'The Changing Face of Representations of Disability in the Media', in J. Swain, S. French and C. Barnes (eds) *Disabling Barriers, Enabling Environments* (London: Sage), pp. 100–105.

Darke, P. (1994) 'The Elephant Man: An Analysis from a Disabled Perspective', *Disability & Society* vol. 9, no. 3, pp. 327–342.

Darke, P. (1998) 'Understanding Cinematic Representation of Disability', in T. Shakespeare (ed.) *The Disability Reader: Social Science Perspectives* (London: Cassell), pp. 181–197.

Darke, P. (1999) *The Cinematic Construction of Physical Disability as Identified Through the Application of the Social Model of Disability to Six Indicative Films Made since 1970*, PhD thesis, University of Warwick. Available at http://www.outside-centre.com/darke/paulphd/content.htm

Davidson, J. (2008) 'Autistic Culture Online: Virtual Communication and Cultural Expression on the Spectrum', *Social & Cultural Geography* vol. 9, pp. 791–806.

Davidson, M. (2010) 'Phantom Limbs: Film Noir and the Disabled Body', in S. Chivers and N. Markotić (eds) *The Problem Body: Projecting Disability on Film* (Columbus, OH: Ohio State University Press), pp. 43–66.

Davis, L. J. (1995) *Enforcing Normalcy: Disability, Deafness, and the Body* (London: Verso).

Davis, L. J. (2000) *My Sense of Silence: Memoirs of a Childhood with Deafness* (Urbana and Chicago, IL: University of Illinois Press).

Davis, L. J. (ed.) (2013) *Disability Studies Reader*, 4th ed. (New York: Routledge)

Dayan, D. and E. Katz (1992) *Media Events: The Live Broadcasting of History* (Cambridge, MA: Harvard University Press).

Deuze, M. (2007) *Media Work* (Cambridge: Polity).

Deuze, M. (ed.) (2011) *Managing Media Work* (Thousand Oaks, CA: Sage).

Diedrich, L. (2005) 'Introduction: Genealogies of Disability', *Cultural Studies* vol. 19, no. 6, pp. 649–666.

Disability Arts Online (2004) 'Caroline Cardus: The Way', *Disability Arts Online*, 1 December. Available at http://www.disabilityartsonline.org.uk/way-ahead

Disability in Action (2014) 'Adriana Macias, A Story of Triumph over Disability', 21st January. Available at http://www.disabilityinaction.com/adriana-macias-a-story-of-triumph-over-disability.html

Downey, G. (2007) 'Constructing Closed-Captioning in the Public Interest: From Minority Media Accessibility to Mainstream Educational Technology', *Info* vol. 9, pp. 69–82.

Dowrick, P. W. and J. Skouge (2001) 'Creating Futures: Potential of Video Empowerment in Postsecondary Education', *Disability Studies Quarterly* vol. 21. Available at http://dsq-sds.org/article/view/255

Drake, S. (2003) 'Disabled Are Fearful: Who Will Be Next?' *LA Times*, 29 October. Available at http://articles.latimes.com/2003/oct/29/news/OE-DRAKE

Drake, S. (2010) 'Fifth Anniversary of Terri Schiavo's Death – A History Lesson', *Not Dead Yet*. Available at http://www.notdeadyet.org/2010/03/fifth-anniversary-of-terri-schiavos.html

Dries, K. (2013) 'Miley's Need to Shock Was the Least Shocking Thing About It.' *Jezebel*, 26 August. Available at http://jezebel.com/mileys-need-to-shock-was-the-least-shocking-thing-abou-1200886682

Effron, M. (ed.) (2011) *The Millennial Detective: Essays on Trends in Crime Fiction, Film and Television, 1990–2010* (Jefferson, NC: McFarland).

Ellcessor, E. (2012) 'Captions On, Off, on TV: Online Accessibility and Search Engine Optimization in Online Closed Captioning', *Television & New Media* vol. 13, no. 4, pp. 329–352.

Ellcessor, E. (2014) '<ALT="Textbooks">: Web Accessibility Myths as Negotiated Industrial Lore' *Critical Studies in Media Communication*, 28 May. DOI: 10.1080/15295036.2014.919660.

Ellis, K. (2008) *Disabling Diversity: The Social Construction of Disability in 1990s Australian National Cinema* (Saarbrücken: VDM-Verlag).

Ellis, K. (2010a) 'Dolls with Disabilities: Playing with Diversity', in N. Norris (ed.) *Unionist Popular Culture and Rolls of Honour in the North of Ireland During the First World War and Other Diverse Essays* (New York: The Edwin Mellen Press), pp. 81–97

Ellis, K. (2010b) 'A Purposeful Rebuilding: YouTube, Representation, Accessibility and the Socio-Political Space of Disability', *Telecommunications Journal of Australia* vol. 60, pp. 21.1–21.12.

Ellis, K. (2011) 'Embracing Learners with Disability: Web 2.0, Access and Insight', *Telecommunications Journal Australia* vol. 61, pp. 30.1–30.11.

Ellis, K. (2012a) 'Complicating a Rudimentary List of Characteristics: Communicating Disability with Down Syndrome Dolls', *M/C Journal* vol. 15, no. 5, http://journal.media-culture.org.au/index.php/mcjournal/article/viewArticle/544

Ellis, K. (2012b) 'It Means Inclusion: A Creative Approach to Disability and Telecommunications Policy in Australia', *Telecommunications Journal Australia* vol. 62, pp. 27.1–27.13.

Ellis, K. (2014) 'Digital Television Flexibility: A Survey of Australians with Disability', *Media International Australia Incorporating Culture and Policy* vol. 96, pp. 96–105.

Ellis, K. (2015) *Disability and Popular Culture: Focusing Passion, Creating Community and Expressing Defiance* (Farnham: Ashgate).

Ellis, K. and M. Kent (2011) *Disability and New Media* (New York: Routledge).

Entman, R. M. (1993) 'Framing: Toward Clarification of a Fractured Paradigm', *Journal of Communication* vol. 43, pp. 51–58.

Entman, R. M. (2007) 'Framing Bias: Media in the Distribution of Power', *Journal of Communication* vol. 57, pp. 163–173.

European Congress on Media and Disability (2003) *European Declaration on Media and Disability*, 14–16 June. Available at http://www.edf-feph.org/page_generale.asp?docid=14476

Finkelstein, V. (1980) *Attitudes and Disabled People: Issues for Discussion* (New York: World Rehabilitation Fund; reprinted London: Radar). Available at http://www.leeds.ac.uk/disability-studies/archiveuk/finkelstein/attitudes.pdf

Flora, G. (2003) 'Improving Media Access for the Hearing-Impaired in Romania and Hungary', in M. Sükösd and P. Bajomi-Lázár (eds) *Reinventing Media: Media Policy Reform in East-Central Europe* (Budapest: Central European University Press), pp. 239–258.

Forde, S. (2011) *Challenging the News: The Journalism of Alternative and Community Media* (Basingstoke: Palgrave Macmillan).

Forsham, B. (2012) *British Crime Film: Subverting the Social Order* (Basingstoke: Palgrave Macmillan).

Fraser, N. (1995) 'From Redistribution to Recognition? Dilemmas of Justice in a 'Post-Socialist Age', *New Left Review* vol. 212, pp. 68–93.

Freeman, H. (2013) 'Miley Cyrus's Twerking Routine was Cultural Appropriation at its Worst', *Guardian*, 27 August. Available at http://www.theguardian.com/commentisfree/2013/aug/27/miley-cyrus-twerking-cultural-appropriation

Fulcher, G. (1989) *Disabling Policies?: A Comparative Approach to Education, Policy, and Disability* (London and New York: Falmer).

Fundación ONCE (2007) *Increasing and Improving Portrayal of People with Disabilities in the Media*. Available http://www.mediaanddisability.org/index.htm

Garland Thomson, R. (ed.) (1996) *Freakery: Cultural Spectacles of the Extraordinary Body* (New York: New York University Press).

Garland Thomson, R. (1997) *Extraordinary Bodies: Figuring Physical Disability in American Culture and Literature* (New York: Columbia University Press).

Garland Thomson, R. (2009) *Staring: How We Look* (Oxford: Oxford University Press).

Gartner, A. and T. Joe (eds) (1986) *Images of the Disabled, Disabling Images* (New York: Praeger).

Gerber, D. (1996) 'The "Careers" of People Exhibited in Freak Shows: The Problem of Volition and Valorization', in R. G. Thomson (ed.), *Freakery: The Cultural Spectacles of the Extraordinary Body* (New York: New York University Press), pp. 38–54.

Germeroth, K. and D. Shultz (1998) 'Should We Laugh or Should We Cry? John Callahan's Humor as a Tool to Change Societal Attitudes Toward Disability', *Howard Journal of Communications* vol. 9, pp. 229–244.

Gilbert, K. and O. J. Schantz (eds) (2008) *The Paralympic Games: Empowerment or Side Show?* (Maidenhead: Meyer & Meyer).

Gilman, G. (2013) 'Web Series "My Gimpy Life" Gets a Second Life Through Kickstarter', *The Wrap*, 13 June. Available at http://tv.yahoo.com/news/series-gimpy-life-gets-second-life-kickstarter-203245143.html.

Ginsburg, F. (2012) 'Disability in the Digital Age', in H. Horst and D. Miller (eds) *Digital Anthropology* (London: Berg), pp. 101–126.

Ginsburg, F. and R. Rapp (2013) 'Disability Worlds', *Annual Review of Anthropology* vol. 42, pp. 53–68.

GLAAD (Gay And Lesbian Alliance Against Defamation) (2010) *Where We Are on TV Report: 2010–2011 Season.* Available at http://www.glaad.org/publications/tvreport10.

GLAAD (2012) *Where We Are on TV: 2012–2013 Season.* Available at http://www.glaad.org/files/whereweareontv12.pdf.

Godley, D. (2011) *Disability Studies: An Interdisciplinary Introduction* (London and Thousand Oaks, CA: Sage).

Godley, D. (2014) *Dis/ability Studies: Theorising Disablism and Ableism* (New York: Routledge).

Godley, D., B. Hughes and L. Davis (eds) (2012) *Disability and Social Theory: New Developments and Directions* (Houndsmill: Palgrave Macmillan).

Goldman, E. (2012) 'Will the Floodgates Open Up for Americans with Disabilities Act (ADA) Claims Against Websites?–National Association of the Deaf v. Netflix', *Technology & Marketing Law Blog*, 26 June. Available at http://blog.ericgoldman.org/archives/2012/06/are_the_floodga.htm

Goggin, G. (2009) 'Disability and the Ethics of Listening', *Continuum* vol. 23, pp. 489–502.

Goggin, G. (2010) '"Laughing at/with the Disabled": The Cultural Politics of Disability in Australian Universities', *Discourse: Studies in the Cultural Politics of Education* vol. 31, pp. 469–481.

Goggin, G. (2015) 'Communication Rights and Disability Online: Policy and Technology after the World Summit on the Information Society (WSIS)', *Information, Communication & Society*, vol. 18, no. 3, pp. 327–341.

Goggin, G. and C. Newell (2000) 'Crippling Paralympics? Media, Disability and Olympism', *Media International Australia* vol. 97, pp. 71–83.

Goggin, G. and C. Newell (2003a) *Digital Disability: The Social Construction of Disability in New Media* (Lanham, MD: Rowman & Littlefield).

Goggin, G. and C. Newell (2003b) 'Imagining Diversity: Disability/Film' Proceedings of the Australian and New Zealand Communications Association

(ANZCA)', *Designing Communication for Diversity* conference, Queensland University of Technology, 9–11 July 2003. Available at http://www.anzca.net/documents/anzca-03-1/refereed-proceedings-7/345-imagining-diversity-disability-film-1.html

Goggin, G. and T. Noonan (2006) 'Blogging Disability: The Interface between New Cultural Movements and Internet Technology', in A. Bruns and J. Jacobs (eds) *Use of Blogs* (New York: Peter Lang), pp. 161–172.

Golfus, B. (2010) 'Billy Golfus, part 09 of 09: Making', *When Billy Broke His Head,* Available at http://www.youtube.com/watch?v=g2GRBHlXtEA

Goodley, D. (2011) *Disability Studies: An Interdisciplinary Introduction* (Los Angeles, CA: Sage).

Goodley, D. (2014) *Dis/ability Studies: Theorising Disablism and Ableism* (London: Routledge).

Goodley, D., B. Hughes and L. Davis (eds) (2012) *Disability and Social Theory: New Developments and Directions* (Basingstoke: Palgrave Macmillan).

Gratton, C., D. Liu, G. Ramchandani and D. Wilson (2012) *The Global Economics of Sport* (New York: Routledge).

Gray, D. (2012) 'Foreword', in D. Moody (ed.) *The Techniques & Etiquette of Community TV production* (Seattle, WA: Amazon Digital Services).

Gray, J. (2008) *Television Entertainment* (New York: Routledge).

Gray, J., J. P. Jones and E. Thompson (eds) (2009) *Satire TV: Politics and Comedy in the Post-Network Era* (New York: NYU Press).

Gregg, M. (2011) *Work's Intimacy* (Cambridge: Polity).

Gripsrud, J., H. Moe, A. Molander and G. Murdock (eds) (2010) *The Idea of the Public Sphere* (Lanham, MD: Lexington).

Hafferty, F. and S. Foster (1994) 'Decontextualizing Disability in the Crime Mystery Genre: The Case of the Invisible Handicap', *Disability & Society* vol. 9, pp. 185–206.

Hall, L (2012) 'Woman in Wheelchair loses Jetstar Appeal', *Sydney Morning Herald,* 23 August. Available at http://www.smh.com.au/travel/travel-news/woman-in-wheelchair-loses-jetstar-appeal-20120823-24ntj.html

Haller, B. (1993) 'The Little Papers Newspapers at 19th Century Schools for Deaf Persons', *Journalism History* vol. 19, no. 2, pp. 42–49.

Haller, B. (2010) *Representing Disability in an Ableist World: Essays on Mass Media* (Louisville, KY: Avocado Press).

Haller, B. and L. Zhang (2010) 'Highlights of 2010 Survey of People with Disabilities about Media Representations', *Media and Disability Resources,* 16 September. Available at http://media-and-disability.blogspot.com.au/2010/09/highlights-of-2010-survey-of-people.html

Harpe, W. (1997) 'Funding the Starters', in A. Pointon and C. Davies (eds) *Framed: Interrogating Disability in the Media* (London: British Film Institute), pp. 147–153.

Harrenstien, K. (2009) 'Automatic Captions in Google', *Google: Official Blog,* 19 November. Available at http://googleblog.blogspot.com.au/2009/11/automatic-captions-in-youtube.html

Hartley, J. (2010) *Digital Futures for Cultural and Media Studies* (New York: Wiley-Blackwell).

Haycraft, H. (1962) 'Books for the Blind: A Postscript and Appreciation', *ALA Bulletin* vol. 56, pp. 795–802.

Hepp, A. (2013) *Cultures of Mediatization* (Cambridge and Malden, MA: Polity).

Hepp, A. and F. Krotz (eds) (2014) *Mediatized Worlds: Culture and Society in a Media Age* (Houndsmill: Palgrave Macmillan).

Henley, L. (2012) 'How Audio-Described TV has Changed My World', *Australian Human Rights Commission*, Available at http://www.humanrights.gov.au/how-audio-described-tv-has-changed-my-world

Hevey, D. (1997) 'Controlling Interests', in A. Pointon and C. Davies (eds) *Framed: Interrogating Disability in the Media* (London: British Film Institute), pp. 209–213.

Hillyer, B. (1993) *Feminism and Disability* (Norman, OK: University of Oklahoma Press).

Hoffman, J. and A. Dakroury (2013) 'Disability Rights between Legal Discourses and Policy Narratives: An Analysis of the European and Canadian Frameworks', *Disability Studies Quarterly* vol. 33, no. 3, http://dsq-sds.org/article/view/1778/3260.

Hollier, S. (2012) *Sociability: Social Media for People with a Disability* (Sydney: Media Access Australia). Available at http://mediaaccess.org.au/online-media/social-media

Hollier, S. (2013) 'Facebook Accessibility: A Year of Progress', Media Access Australia, 9 September. Available at http://mediaaccess.org.au/latest_news/general/facebook-accessibility-a-year-of-progress

Hollywood Life (2013) 'Miley Cyrus Slaps a Twerking Dwarf', *Hollywood Life*, 9 September. Available at https://www.youtube.com/watch?v=wjWmShKSh6M

Holt, J. and K. Sanson (eds) (2014) *Connected Viewing: Selling, Streaming, & Sharing Media in the Digital Age* (London: Routledge).

Honneth, A. (2001) 'Recognition or Redistribution? Changing Perspectives on the Moral Order of Society', *Theory, Culture & Society* vol. 18, pp. 43–55.

Horin, A. (2012) 'Advocate to Appeal Decision on Wheelchair', *Sydney Morning Herald*, 18 January, Available at http://www.smh.com.au/nsw/advocate-to-appeal-decision-on-wheelchair-20120117-1q4sk.html#ixzz2KvfZxiU5

Howe, P. D. (2008) 'From Inside the Newsroom: Paralympic Media and the "Production" of Elite Disability', *International Review for the Sociology of Sport* vol. 43, no. 2, pp. 135–150.

Howley, K. (2010) *Understanding Community Media* (Los Angeles, CA: Sage).

Hutchins, B. and D. Rowe (eds) (2012) *Sport Beyond Television: The Internet, Digital Media and the Rise of Networked Media Sport* (New York: Routledge).

Hutchins, B. and D. Rowe (2013) *Digital Media Sport: Technology, Power and Culture in the Network Society* (New York: Routledge).

Ingstad, B. and S. R. Whyte (eds) (1995) *Disability and Culture* (Berkeley and Los Angeles, CA: University of California Press).

Inimah, G. M., E. Mukulu and P. Mathooko (2012) 'Literature Review on Media Portrayal of People with Disabilities in Kenya', *International Journal of Humanities and Social Science* vol. 2, pp. 223–228.

Institute for the Humanities (2012) 'Two-Day Workshop on Disability and Cross-Sensory Translation', Institute for the Humanities, University of Michigan, Ann Arbor, Michigan, 24 October.

International Labour Organization (ILO) (2010) *Media Guidelines for the Portrayal of Disability* (Geneva: ILO).

International Organization For Standardization (ISO) (2007) 'Signs of the Times – ISO Standard for Universally Understood Public Information Symbols' Available at http://www.iso.org/iso/home/news_index/news_archive/news.htm?refid=Ref1097

International Organization For Standardization (ISO) (2013) *ISO 7001: 2007 Graphical Symbols – Public Information Symbols* (Geneva: ISO)

Ireland, J. (2014) 'Thousands to Lose Disability Support Pension Under Changes Flagged by Government', *Sydney Morning Herald*, 29 June. Available at http://www.smh.com.au/federal-politics/thousands-to-lose-disability-support-pension-under-changes-flagged-by-government-20140629-zspt7.html

Jaeger, P. (2012) *Disability and the Internet: Confronting a Digital Divide* (Boulder, CO and London: Lynne Rienner Publishers).

Jane, H. (2013) 'On Being a Little Person', *A Bunch of Dumb Show* Blog, 9 October. Available at: http://holliseum.wordpress.com/2013/10/09/on-being-a-little-person/

Jansen, S. C., J. Pooley and L. Taub-Pervizpour (eds) (2013) *Media and Social Justice* (New York: Palgrave Macmillan).

Jenkins, H. (2006) *Convergence Culture: Where Old and New Media Collide* (New York: New York University Press)

Jensen, K. B. (ed.) (1998) *News of the World: World Cultures Look at Television News* (London: Routledge).

Joehl, S. (2011) 'A Personal Response to Reed Hastings, Co-Founder & CEO of Netflix', *Accessibility On Demand*, 22 September. Available at https://www.ssbbartgroup.com/blog/2011/09/22/a-personal-response-to-reed-hastings-co-founder-ceo-of-netflix/

Jones, C. (2012) 'Disabled Gulf War Veteran Loses 100 pounds to Prove Doctors Wrong and Walk Again', *Mandatory* 4 May. Available at http://www.mandatory.com/2012/05/04/arthur-boorman-disabled-gulf-war-veteran-loses-100-pounds-prov/

Jones, M. and V. Wass (2013) 'Understanding Disability-Related Employment Gaps in Britain 1998–2011', *Work Employment & Society* vol. 27, pp. 982–1003.

Kama, A. (2004) 'Supercrips Versus the Pitiful Handicapped: Reception of Disabling Images by Disabled Audience Members,' *Communications: The European Journal of Communication Research* vol. 29, pp. 447–466.

Kent, M. and K. Ellis (2013) 'People with Disability and New Disaster Communications: Access and the Social Media Mash-up', *Paper Presented to Global*

Networks – Global Divides: Bringing Traditional and New Communications Challenges, Australian and New Zealand Communication Association (ANZCA) conference, 3–5 July, 2013, Fremantle, Western Australia.

King, D. L. and C. Mele (1999) 'Making Public Access Television: Community, Participation, Media Literacy and the Public Sphere', *Journal of Broadcasting and Electronic Media* vol. 43, pp. 603–623.

Kingett, R. (2014) 'The Accessible Netflix Project Advocates Taking Steps to Ensure Netflix Accessibility for Everyone', *The Accessible Netflix Project*, 26 February. Available at http://netflixproject.wordpress.com/.

Kirkpatrick, B. (2012) '"A Blessed Boon": Radio, Disability, Governmentality, and the Discourse of the "Shut-In", 1920–1930', *Critical Studies in Media Communication* vol. 29, no. 3, pp. 165–184.

Klobas, E. (1988) *Disability Drama in Television and Film* (London: McFarland).

Knox, D. (2009) 'Kristian Schmid on Rafters', 26 August *TV Tonight*, 26 August. Available at http://www.tvtonight.com.au/2009/08/kristian-schmid-on-rafters.html.

Koepsell, D. R. and R. Arp (eds) (2012) *Breaking Bad and Philosophy* (Chicago: Open Court).

Korra (2013) 'Dear Miley, Keep Your Fucking Hands to Yourself,' *GroupThink*, 26 August. Available at http://groupthink.jezebel.com/dear-miley-keep-your-fucking-hands-to-yourself-1201998015.

Kraidy, M. and P. D. Murphy (eds) (2003) *Global Media Studies: An Ethnographic Perspective* (New York: Routledge).

Kubitschke, L., K. Cullen, C. Dolphi, S. Laurin and A. Cederbom (2013) 'Study on Assessing and Promoting E-Accessibility', *European Commission*, Available at http://ec.europa.eu/digital-agenda/en/news/study-assessing-and-promoting-e-accessibility

Kudlick, C. and S. Schweik (2014) 'Collision and Collusion: Artists, Academics, and Activists in Dialogue with the University of California and Critical Disability Studies', *Disability Studies Quarterly* vol. 34, no. 2, http://dsq-sds.org/article/view/4251/3609.

Kuppers, P. (2003) *Disability and Contemporary Performance: Bodies on Edge* (New York: Routledge).

Kuppers, P. (2011) *Disability Culture and Community Performance: Find a Strange and Twisted Shape* (London: Palgrave Macmillan).

Kuppers, P. (2015) *Studying Disability Arts and Culture* (London: Palgrave Macmillan).

Kuusisto, S. (2007) 'A Roundtable on Disability Blogging: Introduction', *Disability Studies Quarterly* vol. 27, no. 1–2, http://www.dsq-sds.org/article/view/1/1.

Ladd, P. (2007) 'Signs of Change: Sign Language and Televisual Media', in M. Cormack and N. Hourigan (eds) *Minority Language Media: Concepts, Critiques and Case Studies* (Clevedon: Multilingual Matters), pp. 248–265.

Lavery, D. (2010) *The Essential Cult TV Reader* (Lexington, KY: University Press of Kentucky).

Law, J. (2014) 'Chronic Diseases that Could be Stamped out Through the Medical Research Future Fund Proposed in Federal Budget 2014', *News.com.au*, 22 May. Available at http://www.news.com.au/lifestyle/health/chronic-diseases-that-could-be-stamped-out-through-the-medical-research-future-fund-proposed-in-federal-budget-2014/

Lazarus, E. (2005) 'Why Congress didn't Help Terri Schiavo's Parents', *CNN.Com*, 31 March. Available at http://edition.cnn.com/2005/LAW/03/31/lazarus.schiavo/index.html?iref=allsearch.

Lebesco, K. (2006) 'Disability, Gender and Difference on The Sopranos', *Women's Studies in Communication* vol. 29, pp. 39–59.

Lefever, K. (2012) *New Media and Sport: International Legal Aspects* (Dordrecht: Springer).

Legg, D. and R. Steadward (2011) 'The Paralympic Games and 60 Years of Change (1948–2008): Unification and Restructuring from a Disability and Medical Model to Sport-Based Competition', *Sports in Society* vol. 14, no. 11, 1099–1115.

Levy, A. (2009) 'The Boy who Never Gave Up: Inspirational Story of How Paralysed Rugby Player Overcame his Disabilities to Win Job at Top Legal Firm,' *Mail Online*, 2 December. Available at http://www.dailymail.co.uk/news/article-1232501/

Lin, J. (2013) 'Farsighted Engineer Invents Bionic Eye to Help the Blind', *UCLA Today*, 21 March. Available at http://today.ucla.edu/portal/ut/wentai-liu-artificial-retina-244393.aspx

Linder, L. R. (1999) *Public Access Television: America's Electronic Soapbox* (Westport, CT: London, Praeger).

Livingstone, S. (1998) 'Audience Research at the Crossroads: The "Implied Audience" in Media and Cultural Theory', *European Journal of Cultural Studies* vol. 1, pp. 193–217.

Livingstone, S. (2009) 'On the Mediation of Everything: ICA Presidential Address 2008', *Journal of Communication* vol. 59, pp. 1–18.

Logan, E. (2013) 'Unacceptability and Prosaic Life in *Breaking Bad*', in J. Potts and J. Scannell (eds) *The Unacceptable* (London and New York: Palgrave Macmillan), pp.156–167.

Longmore, P. (2003) *Why I Burned My Book: and Other Essays on Disability* (Philadelphia, PA: Temple University Press).

Lotz, A. D. (2007) *The Television will be Revolutionized* (New York: New York University Press).

Lubet, A. (2011) *Music, Disability, and Society* (Philadelphia, PA: Temple University Press).

Luther, C. A., C. R. Lepre and N. Clark (2011) *Diversity in U.S. Mass Media* (Chichester, West Sussex: Wiley-Blackwell).

MacBride Commission (1980) *Many Voices, One World: Towards a New, More Just, and More Efficient World Information and Communication Order* (London: Kogan Page).

Macdonald, S. J. and J. Clayton (2012) 'Back to the Future, Disability and the Digital Divide', *Disability & Society* vol. 28, pp. 702–718.

Mackenzie, D. A. and J. Wajcman (1985) *The Social Shaping of Technology: How the Refrigerator Got its Hum* (Milton Keynes and Philadelphia, PA: Open University Press).

Marc, D. (1984) *Demographic Vistas: Television in American Culture* (Philadelphia, PA: University of Pennsylvania Press).

Marr, M. J. (2013) *The Politics of Age and Disability in Contemporary Spanish Film: Plus Ultra Pluralism* (New York: Routledge).

Mckay, A. (2007) *The Official Petition for a More Accessible Facebook*, Available at https://www.facebook.com/groups/2384051749/.

Mckeown, S. and P. Darke (2013) 'Are They Laughing at Us or With Us? Disability in Fox's Animated Series Family Guy', in M. E. Mojk (ed.) *Different Bodies: Essays on Disability in Film and Television* (Jefferson, NC: McFarland), pp. 155–164.

McRuer, R. (2006) *Crip Theory: Cultural Signs of Queerness and Disability* (New York: New York University Press).

Mcruer, R. and A. Mollow (eds) (2012) *Sex and Disability* (Durham, NC: Duke University Press).

Miss Iowa Program (2013) 'Meet Miss Iowa 2013'. Available at http://www.missiowa.com/index.php?option=com_content&view=article&id=176&Itemid=558

Metcalf, G. (2012) *The DVD Novel: How the Way We Watch Television Changed the Television We Watch* (Santa Barbara, CA: Praeger).

Miller, T., G. A. Lawrence, J. Mckay and D. Rowe (2001) *Globalization and Sport: Playing the World* (London: Sage).

Mills, M. (2011a) 'Deafening: Noise and the Engineering of Communication in the Telephone System', *Grey Room* vol. 43, pp. 118–143.

Mills, M. (2011b) 'Do Signals Have Politics? Inscribing Abilities in Cochlear Implants', in T. Pinch and K. Bijsterveld (eds) *The Oxford Handbook of Sound Studies* (Oxford: Oxford University Press), pp. 320–346.

Mills, M. (2011c) 'Hearing Aids and the History of Electronics Miniaturization', *IEEE Annals of the History of Computing* vol. 33, no. 2 (April–June), pp. 24–45.

Mills, M. (2013) 'The Co-Construction of Blindness and Reading', in Ulrike Bergermann (ed.) *Disability Trouble* (Berlin: b_books, 2013), pp. 195–204.

Misener, L. (2013) 'A Media Frames Analysis of the Legacy Discourse for the 2010 Winter Paralympic Games', *Communication & Sport* vol. 1, vol. 4, pp. 342–364.

Mitchell, D. and S. Snyder (eds) (1997) *The Body and Physical Difference: Discourses of Disability* (Ann Arbor, MI: University of Michigan Press).

Mitchell, D. and S. Snyder (2000) *Narrative Prosthesis: Disability and the Dependencies of Discourse* (Ann Arbor, MI: University of Michigan Press).

Mittle, J. (2009) 'Lost in a Great Story: Evaluation in Narrative Television (and Television Studies)', in R. Pearson (ed.) *Reading Lost* (New York: I.B. Tauris), pp. 119–138.

Mojk, M. E. (ed.) (2013) *Different Bodies: Essays on Disability in Film and Television* (Jefferson, NC: McFarland).

MTV (2013) 'Miley Dances With Twerking Dwarf In New Performance', *MTV UK*, 9 September. Available at http://www.mtv.co.uk/news/miley-cyrus/390470-miley-cyrus-twerking-dwarf-performance-snl-host-wrecking-ball-video

Mullin, J. (2012) 'Netflix Settles with Deaf-Rights Group, Agrees to Caption All Videos by 2014', *Arstechnica*, 11 October. Available at http://arstechnica.com/tech-policy/2012/10/netflix-settles-with-deaf-rights-group-agrees-to-caption-all-videos-by-2014/

Müller, F., M. Klijn and L. Van Zoonen (2012) 'Disability, Prejudice and Reality TV: Challenging Disablism through Media Representations', *Telecommunications Journal of Australia* vol. 62, pp. 28.1–28.13.

Morley, D. (2009) 'For a Materialist, Non-Media-Centric Media Studies', *Television & New Media* vol. 10, pp. 114–116.

Moser, I. (2000) 'Against Normalization: Subverting Norms of Ability and Disability', *Science as Culture* vol. 9, no. 2, pp. 201–240.

Moser, I. (2006) 'Disability and the Promises of Technology: Technology, Subjectivity and Embodiment within an Order of the Normal', *Information, Communication & Society* vol. 9, no. 3, pp. 373–395.

Moser, I. and J. Law (2003) 'Making Voices: New Media Technologies, Disabilities, and Articulation', in G. Liestøl, A. Morrison and T. Rasmussen (eds) *Digital Media Revisited: Theoretical and Conceptual Innovation in Digital Domains* (Cambridge, MA & London: MIT Press), pp. 491–520.

My Gimpy Life (2012) 'My Gimpy Announcement!', *YouTube*, 1 February. Available at http://www.youtube.com/watch?v=geucOwiVo0I

Nelson, J. A. (ed.) (1994) *The Disabled, The Media, and The Information Age* (Westport, CT: Greenwood).

Nelson, J. (2000) 'The Media Role in Building the Disability Community', *Journal of Mass Media Ethics* vol. 15, pp. 180–193.

News.com.au (2013) 'Miley Cyrus Spanks Twerking Dwarf on German TV Show *Schlagg Den Raab*', *News.com.au*, 10 September 2013. Available at http://www.news.com.au/entertainment/celebrity-life/miley-cyrus-spanks-twerking-dwarf-on-german-tv-show-schlagg-den-raab/story-e6frfmqi-1226715711836

New York Times (1863) 'The Loving Lilliputians', *New York Times*, 11 February. Available at http://www.nytimes.com/1863/02/11/news/loving-lilliputians-warren-thumbiana-marriage-general-tom-thumb-queen-beauty-who.html?pagewanted=1

NinjaCate (2013) 'Solidarity is For Miley Cyrus: The Racial Implications of her VMA Performance', *GroupThink*, 26 August. Available at http://groupthink.jezebel.com/solidarity-is-for-miley-cyrus-1203666732.

Nomeland, M. M. and R. E. Nomeland (2012) *The Deaf Community in America: History in the Making* (Jefferson, NC: McFarland).

Noonan, M. (2012) 'Managing Manipulation: Tools and Challenges in Creative Collaborations with Intellectually-Disabled People', *Disability & Society* vol. 27, pp. 997–1009.

Norden, M. (1994) *The Cinema of Isolation: A History of Physical Disability in the Movies* (New Brunswick, NJ: Rutgers University Press).

Nye, P. W. (1964) 'Reading Aids for Blind People – A Survey of Progress with the Technological and Human Problems', *Medical Electronics & Biological Engineering* vol. 2, pp. 247–264.

O'Donnell, P., J. Lloyd and T. Dreher (2009) 'Listening, Pathbuilding and Continuations: A Research Agenda for the Analysis of Listening', *Continuum* vol. 23, pp. 423–439.

Ofcom (1998) *Training and Equal Opportunities in ITV, Channel 4, and Channel 5 – 1998* (London: Ofcom). Available at http://www.ofcom.org.uk/static/archive/itc/uploads/Training_&_Equal_Opportunities_in_ITV_Channel_4_and_Channel_51.doc

Ofcom (2011) *The Consumer Experience* (London: Ofcom).

Ofcom (2013) *Television Access Services: Final Report on 2013* (London: Ofcom). Available at http://stakeholders.ofcom.org.uk/market-data-research/market-data/tv-sector-data/tv-access-services-reports/access-services-report-2013/

Oliver, M. (1990) *The Politics of Disablement: A Sociological Approach* (New York: St Martin's Press).

Oliver, M. and C. Barnes (2012) *The New Politics of Disablement* (Basingstoke and New York, NY: Palgrave Macmillan).

Olson, K. (2007) 'Making Connections: Linkages Through Disability Blogging', *Disability Studies Quarterly* vol. 27, no. 1–2, http://www.dsq-sds.org/article/view/6/6.

Padovani, C. and A. Calabrese (eds) (2014) *Communication Rights and Social Justice: Historical Accounts of Transnational Mobilizations* (Basingstoke: Palgrave Macmillan).

Papachrissi, Z. (2010) *A Private Sphere: Democracy in a Digital Age* (Cambridge and Malden, MA, Polity).

Peck, B. and L. T. Kirkbride (2001) 'Why Businesses Don't Employ People with Disabilities', *Journal Vocational Rehabilitation* vol. 16, pp. 71–75.

Pedlow, R. (2008) 'How Will the Changeover to Digital Broadcasting in 2009 Influence the Accessibility of TV for Americans With Disabilities?', *Disability Studies Quarterly* vol. 28, no. 4. Available at http://dsq-sds.org/article/view/130/130

Peers, D. (2009) '(Dis)empowering Paralympic Histories: Absent Athletes and Disabling Discourses', *Disability & Society* vol. 24, no. 5, pp. 653–665.

Philo, G., J. Secker, S. Platt, L. Hendersen, G. Mclaughlin and J. Burnside (1994) 'The Impact of the Mass Media on Public Images of Mental Illness: Media Content and Audience Belief', *Health Education Journal* vol. 53, pp. 271–281.

Pointon, A. and C. Davies (eds) (1997) *Framed: Interrogating Disability in the Media* (London: British Film Institute).

Potter, T. and C. W. Marshall (eds) (2009) *The Wire: Urban Decay and American Television* (New York: Continuum).

Price, M. E. and D. Dayan (eds) (2008) *Owning the Olympics: Narratives of the New China* (Ann Arbor, MI: University of Michigan Press).

Raboy, M. and N. Landry (2005) *Civil Society, Communication and Global Governance: Issues from the World Summit on the Information Society* (New York: Peter Lang).

Rapp, R. and F. Ginsburg (2001) 'Enabling Disability: Renarrating Kinship, Reimagining Citizenship', *Public Culture* vol. 13, no. 3, pp. 533–556.

Raynor, O. and K. Hayward (2005) *The Employment of Performers With Disabilities in the Entertainment Industry*, California: National Arts and Disability Centre, and Screen Actors Guild. Available at http://www.sagaftra.org/files/sag/documents/ExecutiveSummary_PWDReport.pdf

Raynor, O. and K. Hayward (2009) 'Breaking into the Business: Experiences of Actors with Disabilities in the Entertainment Industry', *Journal of Research in Special Educational Needs* vol. 9, pp. 39–47.

RCA (1937) 'RCA Advertising: How the Blind "Read" with their Ears', *Life* 11 October, p. 5.

Rennie, E. (2006) *Community Media: A Global Introduction* (Lanham, MD: Rowman & Littlefield).

Riddell, S. and N. Watson (2003) 'Disability, Culture and Identity: An Introduction', in S. Riddell and N. Watson (eds) *Disability, Culture & Identity* (London: Routledge), pp. 1–18.

Riley, C. (2005) *Disability and the Media: Prescriptions for Change* (Lebanon, NH: University Press of New England).

Rizzo, C. (2013) 'Glee Project Star Ali Stroker on Artie's Love Life – Exclusive', *Wetpaint Glee*, Available at http://www.wetpaint.com/glee/articles/glee-project-star-ali-stroker-on-arties-love-life-exclusive

Roberts, P. (1997) 'Getting into Video', in A. Pointon and C. Davies (eds) *Framed: Interrogating Disability in the Media* (London: British Film Institute), pp. 144–146.

Robertson, J. (2013) 'Miley Cyrus Hires Dwarves to Recreate Controversial Twerking Performance at her 21st Birthday Party,' *Mirror.co.uk*, 25 November. Available at http://www.mirror.co.uk/3am/celebrity-news/video-miley-cyrus-twerking-dwarves-2850057

Rodan, D., K. Ellis and P. Lebeck (2014) *Disability, Obesity and Ageing: Popular Media Identifications* (Farnham: Ashgate).

Ross, K. (1997) 'But Where's Me in It? Disability, Broadcasting and the Audience', *Media Culture Society* vol. 19, pp. 669–677.

Rowe, D. (2012) *Global Media Sport: Forms, Flows and Futures* (New York: Bloomsbury).

Rubin, L. C. (ed.) (2012) *Mental Illness in Popular Media: Essays on the Representation of Disorders* (Jefferson, NC: McFarland).

Ryan, F. (2012) 'The Last Leg: Often Tasteless, Sometimes Awkward, Always Funny', *Guardian*, 5 September. Available at http://www.guardian.co.uk/tv-and-radio/tvandradioblog/2012/sep/05/the-last-leg-tasteless-awkward-funny.

Saito, S. and R. Ishiyama (2005) 'The Invisible Minority: Under-Representation of People with Disabilities in Prime-Time TV Dramas in Japan', *Disability & Society* vol. 20, pp. 437–451.

Sanchez, J. (2012) 'The ADA and the Internet', *Cato At Liberty*, 29 June. Available at http://www.cato.org/blog/ada-internet.

Sancho, J. (2003) *Disabling Prejudice? Attitudes Towards Disability and its Portrayal on Television, A report of research undertaken by the British Broadcasting Corporation, the Broadcasting Standards Commission and the Independent Television Commission.* Available at http://downloads.bbc.co.uk/guidelines/editorialguidelines/research/disabling-prejudice.pdf

Sandahl, C. and P. Auslander (2005) *Bodies in Commotion: Disability and Performance* (Ann Arbor, MI: University of Michigan Press).

Sapey, B. (2000) 'Disablement in the Information Age', *Disability & Society* vol. 15, pp. 619–637.

Sassen, S. (ed.) (2007) *Deciphering the Global: Its Scales, Spaces and Subjects* (New York: Routledge).

Scannell, P. (ed.) (1991) *Broadcast Talk* (London: Sage).

Schlesinger, P. (1985) 'From Public Service to Commodity: The Political Economy of Teletext in the UK', *Media, Culture & Society* vol. 7, pp. 471–485.

Schweik, S. (2012) Available at http://events.umich.edu/event/10429-1174116

Scorsese, M. (dir.) (2013) *The Wolf of Wall Street.*

Sepinwall, A. (2012) *The Revolution was Televised: The Cops, Crooks, Slingers and Slayers Who Changed TV Drama Forever* (Austin, TX: Touchstone).

Servaes, J. and N. Carpentier (eds.) (2006) *Towards a Sustainable European Information Society* (Bristol: Intellect).

Shakespeare, T. (1994) 'Cultural Representation of Disabled People: Dustbins for Disavowal?', *Disability & Society* vol. 9, pp. 283–299.

Shakespeare, T. (2006) *Disability Rights and Wrongs* (London and New York: Routledge).

Shakespeare, T. (2009) 'Not Just a Pretty Facebook', *Ouch!*, Available at http://www.bbc.co.uk/ouch/opinion/not_just_a_pretty_facebook.shtml

Shaw, M. (2010) ''The Specials' Shows Life with Special Needs, Especially Watchable', *Tube Filter*, 2 June. Available at http://www.tubefilter.com/2010/06/02/the-specials-shows-life-with-special-needs-especially-watchable/

Sherer, T. (2013) 'Kickstarter Projects: *My Gimpy Life* Season 2', *Kickstarter*, 15 June. Available at http://www.kickstarter.com/projects/1993187916/my-gimpy-life-season-two.

Sherry, M. (2013) 'Crip Politics? Just...No', *The Feminist Wire*, 23 November. Available at http://thefeministwire.com/2013/11/crip-politics-just-no/

Shildrick, M. (2009) *Dangerous Discourses of Disability, Subjectivity and Sexuality* (Basingstoke: Palgrave Macmillan).

Siebers, T. (2008) *Disability Theory* (Ann Arbor, MI: University of Michigan Press).

Siebers, T. (2010) *Disability Aesthetics* (Ann Arbor, MI: University of Michigan Press).

Silvers, A., D. Wasserman and M. B. Mahowald (1998) *Disability, Difference, Discrimination: Perspectives on Justice in Bioethics and Public Policy* (Lanham, MD: Rowman & Littlefield).

Silva, C. F. and P. D. Howe (2012) 'The (In)validity of *Supercrip* Representation of Paralympian Athletes', *Journal of Sport and Social Issues* vol. 36, pp. 174–194

Silverstone, R. (2004) *Television and Everyday Life* (London and New York: Routledge).

Silverstone, R. (2007) *Media and Morality: On the Rise of the Mediapolis* (Cambridge and Malden, MA: Polity).

Sinclair, S., G. Bramley, L. Dobbie and M. Gillespie (2007) *Social Inclusion and Communications: A Review of the Literature* (London: Ofcom). Available at http://www.communicationsconsumerpanel.org.uk/downloads/Research/LowIncomeConsumers_Research/Social%20inclusion%20and%20communications/Social%20inclusion%20and%20communications.pdf

Slater, J., J-I. Lindström and G. Astbrink (2010) *Broadband Solutions for Consumers with Disabilities* (Sydney: ACCAN).

Smart, G. (2013) 'Miley Cyrus Hard at Twerk Again...This Time with a Dwarf', *The Sun*, 14 September, http://www.thesun.co.uk/sol/homepage/showbiz/bizarre/5134046/miley-cyrus-twerks-with-dwarf-at-sony-gig.html

Smit, C. R. and A. Enns (eds) (2001) *Screening Disability: Essays on Cinema and Disability* (Lanham, MD: University Press of America).

Smith, A. (2012) *Hideous Progeny: Disability, Eugenics, and Classic Horror Cinema* (New York: Columbia University Press).

Snyder, S. L. and D. Mitchell (2006) *Cultural Locations of Disability* (Chicago, IL, University of Chicago Press).

Spacecrip (2012) '*Twin Peaks*: Manufacturing Quirkiness ...and Danger', *Space Crip*, 23 July. Available at http://spacecrip.wordpress.com/2012/07/23/twin-peaks-manufacturing-quirkiness-and-danger/.

Sparks, R. (1992) *Television and the Drama of Crime: Moral Tales and the Place of Crime in Public Life* (Buckingham and Philadelphia, PA: Open University Press).

Spence, E. H., A. Alexandra, A. Quinn and A. Dunn (2011) *Media, Markets, and Morals* (Malden, MA: John Wiley).

Springer, K. (2012) 'Watch: Disabled Veteran Does the Impossible', *Time*, 10 May. Available at http://newsfeed.time.com/2012/05/10/watch-disabled-veteran-does-the-impossible/

State Journal (2013) 'Franklin County Woman Accused of Taking $20,000 from Disabled Veterans', *The State Journal*, (Frankfort, KY), 16 August. Available at: http://www.state-journal.com/latest%20headlines/2013/08/16/franklin-county-woman-accused-of-taking-20-000-from-disabled-veteran

Sterne, J. and D. Mulvin (2014) 'The Low Acuity for Blue: Perceptual Technics and American Color Television', *Journal of Visual Culture* vol. 13, no. 2, pp. 118–138.

Straus, J. (2011) *Extraordinary Measures: Disability in Music* (Oxford: Oxford University Press).

Swain, J., S. French, C. Barnes and C. Thomas (eds) (2014) *Disabling Barriers – Enabling Environments*, 3rd edition (London and Los Angeles, CA: Sage).

Taylor, A. (2012) 'London 2012: The Opening Ceremony', *The Atlantic*, 28 July. Available at http://www.theatlantic.com/infocus/2012/07/london-2012-the-opening-ceremony/100343/

Taylor, C. (2003) *Modern Social Imaginaries* (Durham, NC: Duke University Press).

Tester, K. (2001) *Compassion, Morality and the Media* (Buckingham: Open University).

The Glee Project Wiki (2013) 'Blake Jenner'. Available at http://thegleeproject. wikia.com/wiki/Blake_Jenner

The Goldfish (2007) 'Blogging Brings More of Us to the Table', *Disability Studies Quarterly* vol. 27, pp. 1–2, http://www.dsq-sds.org/article/view/4/4.

Thomas, N. and A. Smith (2009) *Disability, Sport and Society: An Introduction* (London and New York: Routledge).

Thoreau, E. (2006) 'Ouch!: An Examination of the Self-Representation of Disabled People on the Internet', *Journal of Computer-Mediated Communication* vol. 11, http://jcmc.indiana.edu/vol11/issue2/thoreau.html.

Titchkovsky, T. (2011) *The Question of Access: Disability, Space, Meaning* (Toronto, ON: University of Toronto Press).

Tomlinson, A. and C. Young (eds) (2005) *National Identity and Global Sports Events: Culture, Politics, and Spectacle in the Olympics and the Football World Cup* (Albany, NY: State University of New York Press).

Townsend, P. (1966) 'Foreword', in P. Hunt (ed.) *Stigma: The Experience of Disability*. London: Geoffrey Chapman. Available at http://disability-studies.leeds.ac. uk/files/library/Hunt-Foreword.pdf

Tremain, S. (ed.) (2005) *Foucault and the Government of Disability* (Ann Arbor, MI: University of Michigan Press)

Turner, G. (2007) 'Some Things We Should Know About Talkback Radio', *Media International Australia* vol. 122, pp. 73–80.

Turner, G. (2009) *Ordinary People and the Media: The Demotic Turn* (London: Sage).

Turner, G. (2013) *Understanding Celebrity*, 2nd edition (London: Sage).

Tzanelli, R. (2013) *Olympic Ceremonialism and the Performance of National Character: From London 2012 to Rio 2016* (Basingstoke: Palgrave Macmillan).

Utray, F., M. de Castro, L. Moreno and B. E. Ruiz-Mezcua (2012) 'Monitoring Accessibility Services in Digital Television', *International Journal of Digital Multimedia Broadcasting* vol. 2012, Article ID 294219, 9 pages, 2012. doi:10.1155/2012/294219, http://dx.doi.org/10.1155/2012/294219.

Various (2013) '573 Responses to "On Being a Little Person," ' *A Bunch of Dumb Show* blog, 9 October. Available at http://holliseum.wordpress.com/2013/10/09/on-being-a-little-person/.

Vasey, S. (2004) 'Disability Culture: The Story So Far', in J. Swain, S. French and C. Barnes (eds) *Disabling Barriers, Enabling Environments* (London: Sage), pp. 106–110.

Visentin, L. (2014) 'Jetstar Business Model Leaves Jim Conway Stuck in Wheelchair', *Sydney Morning Herald*, 14 June, http://www.smh.com.au/nsw/

jetstar-business-model-leaves-jim-conway-stuck-in-wheelchair-20140614-zs7vr.html

Walker, A., A. Sinfield and C. Walker (eds) (2011) *Fighting Poverty, Inequality and Injustice: A Manifesto Inspired by Peter Townsend* (Bristol: The Policy Press).

Wark, K. (1994) *Virtual Geography: Living with Global Media Events* (Bloomington, IN: Indiana University Press).

Warren, N. and L. Manderson (eds) (2013) *Reframing Disability and Quality of Life: A Global Perspective* (Dordrecht: Springer).

Watson, N., A. Roulstone and C. Thomas (eds) (2012) *Routledge Handbook of Disability Studies* (New York: Routledge).

Watermeyer, B. (2012) *Towards a Contextual Psychology of Disablism* (London: Routledge).

Weber, I. and V. Evans (2002) 'Constructing the Meaning of Digital Television in Britain, the United States and Australia', *New Media & Society* vol.4, pp. 435–456.

Weissmann, E. (2012) *Transnational Television Drama* (Basingstoke: Palgrave Macmillan).

West, B. and S. Gandhi (2006) 'Reporting Abuse: A Study of the Perceptions of People with Disabilities (PWD) Regarding Abuse Directed at PWD', *Disability Studies Quarterly* vol. 26, http://dsq-sds.org/article/view/650/827.

Wilde, A. (2004) 'Are You Sitting Comfortably? Soap Operas, Disability and Audience?,' Available at http://disability-studies.leeds.ac.uk/files/library/wilde-Alison-Wilde-Dis-cover-2-Adapted-Paper.pdf

Wildman, S. (2013) 'An Open Letter to Netflix RE: Subtitles', *Nerdophiles*, 13 August. Available at http://nerdophiles.com/2013/08/13/an-open-letter-to-netflix-re-subtitles/

Williamson, K., D. Schauder and A. Bow (2000) 'Information Seeking by Blind and Sight Impaired Citizens: An Ecological Study', *Information Research* vol. 5, no. 4, http://informationr.net/ir/5–4/paper79.html.

Wilson, J. C. and C. Lewiecki-Wilson (eds) (2001) *Embodied Rhetorics: Disability in Language and Culture* (Carbondale, IL: Southern Illinois University Press).

Wiser, D. (2013) 'Fraudulent Disability Claims Threatening Social Security Program: $21b in False Disability Claims', *Fox News*, 27 June. Available at http://nation.foxnews.com/2013/06/27/report-21b-false-disability-claims-handed-out-annually

Wodak, R. and V. Koller (eds) (2008) *Handbook of Communication in the Public Sphere* (Berlin: Mouton de Gruyter).

Wolford, J. (2012) 'Netflix Will Caption All Streaming Videos by 2014, Per Settlement', *WebProNews/ Technology*, 11 October. Available at http://www.webpronews.com/netflix-will-caption-all-streaming-videos-by-2014-per-settlement-2012-10

Wollheim, P. (2007) 'The Erratic Front: YouTube and Representations of Mental Illness', *Afterimage*, September–October vol. 35, no. 2, pp. 21, 24–26.

Wood, L. (2012) 'Media Representation of Disabled People', website. Available at http://www.disabilityplanet.co.uk/index.html

World Health Organization (WHO) (2001) *International Classification of Functioning, Disability and Health* (Geneva: WHO).

World Health Organization (WHO) (2011) *World Report on Disability* (Geneva: WHO). Available at http://www.who.int/disabilities/world_report/2011/en/

Young, S. (2012) 'We're Not Here for Your Inspiration', *Ramp Up*, 2 July. Available at http://www.abc.net.au/rampup/articles/2012/07/02/3537035.htm

Druidshills 2005 (2013) 'Inspirational Disabled Children', *YouTube* playlist. Available at https://www.youtube.com/playlist?list=PL6F11030A584517FA

Zajicek, M. (2007) 'Keynote Address: Web 2.0: Hype or Happiness?' 16th International World Wide Web Conference, 7–8 May, Banff, Canada.

Zola, I. K. (1985) 'Depictions of Disability – Metaphor, Message, and Medium in the Media: A Research and Political Agenda', *The Social Science Journal* vol. 22, no. 4, pp. 5–17.

Zola, I. K. (1987) 'Any Distinguishing Features? The Portrayal of Disability in the Crime-Mystery Genre', *Policy Studies Journal* vol. 15, pp. 485–513.

Zola, I. K. (1989) 'Towards the Necessary Universalizing of a Disability Policy', *Milbank Quarterly* vol. 67, pp. 401–428.

Index

Printed by Printforce, the Netherlands